Cambridge Opera Handbooks

W. A. Mozart
La clemenza di Tito

CAMBRIDGE OPERA HANDBOOKS
Published titles

W. A. Mozart
La clemenza di Tito

JOHN A. RICE

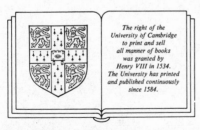

The right of the
University of Cambridge
to print and sell
all manner of books
was granted by
Henry VIII in 1534.
The University has printed
and published continuously
since 1584.

CAMBRIDGE UNIVERSITY PRESS

Cambridge
New York   Port Chester
Melbourne   Sydney

Published by the Press Syndicate of the University of Cambridge
The Pitt Building, Trumpington Street, Cambridge CB2 1RP
40 West 20th Street, New York, NY 10011–4211, USA
10 Stamford Road, Oakleigh, Melbourne 3166, Australia

First published 1991

Printed in Great Britain at the University Press, Cambridge

British Library cataloguing in publication data
Rice, John A.
    W. A. Mozart, La clemenza di Tito.   (Cambridge opera handbooks).
    1. Opera in Italian. Mozart, Wolfgang Amadeus, 1756–1791
    I. Title
    782.1092

Library of Congress cataloguing in publication data
Rice, John A.
    W. A. Mozart, La clemenza di Tito/ John A. Rice.
        p.   ca. – (Cambridge opera handbooks)
    Includes bibliographical references
    Discography: p.
    ISBN 0 521 36142 7. ISBN 0 521 36949 5 (pbk.)
    I. Mozart, Wolfgang Amadeus, 1756–1791. Clemenza di Tito.
    II. Title.   III. Series.
    ML410.M9R54   1991
    782.1–dc20   90-2068   CIP MN

ISBN 0 521 36142 7 hardback
ISBN 0 521 36949 5 paperback

CE

To the memory of my mother
Charlotte Rice, née Bloch
Prague 1918 – New York 1982

Contents

Illustrations

viii

General preface

This is a series of studies of individual operas, written for the serious opera-goer or record-collector as well as the student or scholar. Each volume has three main concerns. The first is historical: to describe the genesis of the work, its sources or its relation to literary prototypes, the collaboration between librettist and composer, and the first performance and subsequent stage history. This history is itself a record of changing attitudes towards the work, and an index of general changes of taste. The second is analytical and it is grounded in a very full synopsis which considers the opera as a structure of musical and dramatic effects. In most volumes there is also a musical analysis of a section of the score, showing how the music serves or makes the drama. The analysis, like the history, naturally raises questions of interpretation, and the third concern of each volume is to show how critical writing about an opera, like production and performance, can direct or distort appreciation of its structural elements. Some conflict of interpretation is an inevitable part of this account; editors of the handbooks reflect this – by citing classic statements, by commissioning new essays, by taking up their own critical position. A final section gives a select bibliography, a discography and guides to other sources.

Acknowledgments

This book has benefitted much from the careful reading and thoughtful criticism of Ron Caldwell, John S. Powell and Eugene F. Rice. Brian Newhouse, who first suggested that I write this book, read the proofs four years later. John Gibbs and Eric Offenbacher helped me compile the discography. David Wood made available to me the resources of the Music Library, University of Washington, where I spent many pleasant hours of research. Daniel Heartz, as teacher, scholar and friend, inspired and sustained my interest in *La clemenza di Tito*.

The illustrations appear by permission of the following: Plate 1, National Gallery, Prague; Plate 2, Historisches Museum, Frankfurt am Main; Plate 3, Vatican Museum, Vatican City; Plate 4, Harry Ransom Humanities Research Center, University of Texas, Austin; Plate 5, State Library, Prague; Plates 6, 7, 8 and 13, Winnie Klotz, Metropolitan Opera, New York; Plate 9, Theatermuseum, Universität Köln, Cologne; Plate 10, Museo Teatrale alla Scala, Milan; Plate 11, Boston Symphony Orchestra Archives (photo by Will Plouffe Studio); Plate 12, Unitel Film- und Fernseh-Produktionsgesellschaft, Munich; Plate 14, Drottningholms Slottsteater; Plate 15, Agence de Presse Bernand, Paris.

A coronation opera for the German Titus

When Leopold II (Plate 1) came to the Habsburg throne in February 1790 he found the monarchy in crisis. An unpopular war against the Turks had dragged on much longer than anyone had expected. War taxes and forced conscription caused discontent among the peasants and middle classes. The powerful nobility of Bohemia and Hungary, frustrated by constant efforts of Joseph II, Leopold's older brother and predecessor, to increase the central government's authority at their expense and alarmed by his attempts to better the peasants' lot, threatened to rebel. The Hungarian nobility had succeeded in convincing Joseph, on his death-bed, to revoke some of his most important reforms. But even with these concessions in hand some Hungarians continued to prepare for armed resistance; and the Prussians, old enemies of the Habsburg monarchy, threatened to come to the aid of the Hungarian nobility. Already the Austrian Netherlands were in revolt, having declared themselves an independent republic, the United States of Belgium, on 20 January 1790. The outbreak of the French Revolution in the previous year represented a dangerous and ultimately fatal challenge not only to the French monarchy, closely allied to the Habsburgs by marriage, but also to the tradition of absolute monarchy in general.[1]

Leopold had reigned in Florence as Grand Duke of Tuscany since 1765. He had become an experienced and skillful ruler during his twenty-five years in Italy. Now forty-three years old, he arrived in Vienna eager to attack the problems facing the monarchy, and capable of doing so. An important element in his response to the crisis was the use of carefully chosen concessions to appease and to win over various groups adversely affected by Joseph's reforms. By means of these concessions Leopold was able to divide and thus to weaken the opposition. At the same time his government began an ideological offensive against the French Revolution and its

1

1   Emperor Leopold II. Portrait, possibly unfinished, by H. F. Füger,
c. 1791

supporters within the Habsburg monarchy: a vigorous campaign to
portray the Revolution as wicked and destructive and to justify the
assumptions underlying enlightened absolutism.

Leopold consolidated power slowly, a process manifested in a
series of coronations: as Emperor of the Holy Roman Empire
(October 1790), as King of Hungary (November 1790), and as King

of Bohemia (September 1791). These coronations were opportunities to affirm, through the powerful symbolism of the coronation ritual, the strength and resilience of enlightened absolutism, opportunities for Leopold to bask in the warmth of pomp and applause, to celebrate and to renew the traditions of the political system that kept him in power. For those over whom Leopold ruled these coronations were opportunities too: not only to applaud their new sovereign, but also to display their own traditions, to demonstrate that they were consenting freely to be ruled by Leopold and that such consent came in exchange for Leopold's recognition that they had certain rights and privileges.

Like most eighteenth-century coronations, Leopold's coronations were patently theatrical: they were dramas whose casts included the Habsburg monarchy's richest and most powerful actors. The sovereign himself had the leading role. An engraving inspired by Leopold's coronation at Frankfurt evokes the theatrical atmosphere of Leopold's coronations (Plate 2). An allegorical figure of Germany offers the hearts of her people to the newly-crowned emperor, as Fame, flying above, trumpets the name of

2 "Vivat Leopoldus Secundus." Allegorical engraving by I. C. Berndt in celebration of Leopold's coronation as Emperor of the Holy Roman Empire, 1790

Leopold to the rising sun. The foreground is a stage on which Leopold and the personification of Germany appear as if actors. Fame, like a theatrical *dea ex machina*, seems to be held aloft by a cloud machine of the kind used often in eighteenth-century opera. In the background the people of Germany assemble, like an audience in the theater, to witness the spectacle acted out before them. (They embrace one another, as if to show that the French Revolution had no monopoly on *fraternité*).

In keeping with the theatrical quality of eighteenth-century coronations, the production of plays and operas was an essential part of the festivities surrounding most coronations; Leopold's coronations were no exception. In Frankfurt performances included at least one play and two operas. In Prague at least three operas were performed in the days before and after Leopold's coronation as King of Bohemia.[2] But the main theatrical event in Prague was the premiere of a new serious opera on the evening of coronation day, 6 September 1791: *La clemenza di Tito*, with poetry by Pietro Metastasio, as revised by Caterino Mazzolà, and music by Wolfgang Amadeus Mozart.

The opera had been conceived and executed in haste. Representatives of the Bohemian Estates (which meant, for all practical purposes, representatives of the Bohemian nobility and the Catholic Church) had been called into session by Leopold during the summer of 1790. The so-called "Big Bohemian Diet" of 1790–91 was an extraordinary event, paralleling in some respects the pre-revolutionary conventions of the French Estates called together by Louis XVI.[3] The representatives assembled in Prague worked through the second half of 1790 and the first month of 1791 preparing "Desideria" addressed to Leopold as King of Bohemia: requests for legislation and other actions by Leopold – most of them, in effect, concessions – concerning taxation, serfdom, the Bohemian constitution, and other issues related to the kingdom of Bohemia. The Diet of the Estates met again several times later in 1791; the last of their meetings that year took place in June, and it was presumably during this meeting that the Estates decided to celebrate Leopold's upcoming coronation with a sumptuous and expensive opera.

On 8 July 1791, a little less than two months before the coronation, Domenico Guardasoni, impresario of the Italian opera in Prague, concluded an agreement with the Estates of Bohemia in which he promised to provide an opera as part of the coronation

festivities. The contract is signed by Guardasoni, by Count Heinrich Rottenhan, *Burggraf* (Governor) of Bohemia, and by four
members of the Diet.[4] Governor Rottenhan presided over the Diet
and represented the interests not of the Bohemian Estates, but of
the central government in Vienna; he was, in other words, Leopold's principal agent in Prague. Rottenhan was a skillful politician, adept at the difficult task of representing Leopold before the
Diet diplomatically and yet firmly. "He possessed those qualities
which Cavriani [the previous governor] lacked," one historian of
the period has written, "namely a glib tongue to lull the Estates and
tact to soothe them into believing that the government was going to
do something entirely different from what it intended."[5] Rottenhan
may well have played a crucial role in the negotiations that led to
the operatic commission, for it was in his interest especially that
Leopold's coronation be as brilliant and impressive as possible.
When the opera was performed on coronation day, Rottenhan sat
with Leopold and his family in the royal box.

Guardasoni's contract tells us much about how the opera was
organized. Here is a translation of the document, the original of
which, in Italian, is in the State Archives in Prague:

Specification of the points that I the undersigned promise the High Estates
of Bohemia to honor [unintelligible phrase omitted] concerning a grand
opera seria to be presented in this National Theater on the occasion of the
coronation of His Imperial Majesty, within the first days of September
next, at which time I shall be paid six thousand florins, or six thousand five
hundred if the *musico* should be Marchesi.

1. I promise to give them [i.e. the Estates] a *primo musico* of the first rank
   such as, for example, Marchesini [i.e. Luigi Marchesi], or [Giovanni]
   Rubinelli, or [Girolamo] Crescentini, or [Valeriano] Violani, or
   another, as long he be of the first rank.
   Likewise I promise to give them a *prima donna*, likewise of the first
   rank and certainly the best of that level free of other engagements, and
   to hire from my company the rest of the singers necessary for the
   opera.
2. I promise to have the poetry of the libretto composed on [one of] the
   two subjects given to me by His Excellence the Burgrave [i.e.
   Governor Rottenhan] and to have it set to music by a distinguished
   composer; but in the case it should not be at all possible to accomplish
   this in the short time remaining, I promise to procure an opera newly
   composed on the subject of Metastasio's *Tito*.
3. I promise to have two new changes of scenery made expressly for this
   spectacle.
   . Likewise I promise to have new costumes made, and especially for
   the leading roles in the opera.

4. I promise to illuminate and to decorate the theater with garlands, to present the said opera complete, and to perform it gratis for one evening, to be specified by the High Estates, within the above-mentioned time.

Important points:

1. That I will be lent six hundred florins for my trip to Vienna and to Italy, on an order payable by a banker in Vienna and in Italy, and that I will be given some two thousand florins there, in case those engaged should ask for advances.
2. That the rest of the payment will be made to me on the day on which the said opera is performed.
3. If in the space of 14 days from the day of my departure for Italy the opera should be cancelled, only the expenses of the trip will be paid.
4. Guardasoni will announce at once the day on which he has engaged a virtuoso; if the opera is cancelled, this virtuoso will be reimbursed if he has already left Italy.
5. If the opera should be cancelled the things bought with the money that has been advanced are to be returned and the money refunded, and contracts not yet closed are to be annulled, and Guardasoni will be given remuneration if he proves that his travel expenses exceeded his advance.

Prague, 8 July 1791

> Henrico Conte di Rottenhan
> Casparo Ermanno Conte Kinigl [Künigl]
> Giuseppe Conte di Sweerth
> Giovanni Conte Unwerth
> Giovanni Baron d'Hennet

> > Domenico Guardasoni
> > Impresario

The contract specifies Guardasoni's fee as 6000 florins, or 6500, "if the *musico* should be Marchesi." *Musico* was the normal eighteenth-century term for a castrated male soprano or contralto. (The term *castrato*, common today, usually had derogatory implications when applied to singers in the eighteenth century.) Luigi Marchesi was one of the greatest *musici* of the day. From this and other stipulations of the contract we can conclude that Guardasoni was to pay all expenses – singers' fees as well as those of librettist, composer, designer, and painter of the scenery – out of the sum that he was to receive.

The contract makes clear that Count Rottenhan and the Bohemian Estates wanted their opera to be as lavish as possible, at least insofar as the quality of the leading singers was concerned. Yet it is interesting to note that the contract mentions only two roles, the *primo musico* and the *prima donna*; no mention is made of first tenor, who in most eighteenth-century *opere serie* had a role that rivalled, if not equalled, in musical and dramatic importance those of the *primo musico* and *prima donna*. Guardasoni took advantage of this lack of specificity by hiring a member of his own company for this tenor role.

Guardasoni was free, according to his contract, to choose whatever composer he wished for the coronation opera, as long as the composer was "un cellebre maestro." Clearly the composer was not the most pressing concern either for the commissioners of the opera or for its organizer. We will see in chapter 4 that Guardasoni made every effort to engage "a distinguished composer" to write the music. After failing with his first choice, Antonio Salieri, he succeeded with his second.

La clemenza di Tito and the return of *opera seria* to Vienna

Guardasoni's contract calls specifically for "una grand'opera seria." By "opera seria," a term that came into general use in the last quarter of the eighteenth century, he meant a *dramma per musica*. The typical *dramma per musica* was a full-length opera with a serious, usually historical or pseudo-historical plot, with a cast consisting of six or seven characters of royal or noble birth. *Opera seria* of this kind was the century's most prestigious and costly genre of musical theater, a genre often called for on special occasions – inaugurations of theaters, visits of foreign dignitaries, state weddings, and, of course, coronations. At the same time *opera seria* was also a regular part of the musical life, a staple of the repertory, in every one of Italy's major operatic centers and in several operatic centers elsewhere in Europe.

Opera seria has come in for more than its fair share of ridicule and condescension over the last two centuries. "The decline of *opera seria*" is a process that historians have noted throughout the history of the genre. Benedetto Marcello's satirical "Teatro alla moda" (1720), the failure of Handel's serious operas in London during the 1730s, the success of Gluck's reform operas during the 1760s, the popularity of opera buffa in the second half of the eighteenth century: all of these have been interpreted as symptoms or reflections of "the decline of *opera seria*." Musicians have wondered why Mozart would have had anything to do with a dying genre; many have concluded that he wrote *La clemenza di Tito* against his will, and only because he needed the money.

In fact, as much recent musical scholarship has shown, *opera seria* was hardly dead in 1791. It continued to thrive in Italy. And it continued to thrive in some of northern Europe's operatic centers, including London and Berlin. Far from approaching extinction, *opera seria* was gradually evolving – developing into the type of serious opera we are familiar with from examples by Rossini, Donizetti, and Bellini.[6]

But the decision to celebrate the coronation of a Habsburg monarch with an *opera seria* is nevertheless an event that calls for attention and explanation. However popular it was in many parts of Europe, *opera seria* was not in official favor in Vienna during the 1780s. Its absence from the stage of the Burgtheater was in part a matter of the tastes of Emperor Joseph II, who claimed that he found the genre boring (he may also have found it too expensive).[7] Since the Habsburg court reserved for itself the privilege of staging operas within the walls of Vienna during the eighteenth century, the Emperor's tastes greatly influenced the city's operatic life. The 1780s produced great achievements in the realm of comic opera in Vienna; but, as we might guess from Joseph's attitude, little was accomplished in serious opera.

This situation affected every composer writing operas in Vienna during the 1780s. The Spaniard Vicente Martín y Soler was one such composer. Before coming to Vienna in 1785 Martín spent several years composing operas in Italy, where, like many of his Italian colleagues, he divided his time about equally between *opera buffa* and *opera seria*; he wrote at least four serious operas between 1779 and 1783. But in Vienna he wrote only comic operas, the most popular being *Una cosa rara* (1786) and *L'arbore di Diana* (1787), both to librettos by Lorenzo Da Ponte. Martín was so successful with comic opera in Vienna that for the rest of his career he devoted most of his compositional efforts to comic opera, even when composing for London, where *opera seria* continued to enjoy favor along with *opera buffa*.

During the first year of Leopold's reign operatic repertory in the Burgtheater continued along the lines laid out during Joseph's reign: only comic operas were performed. Among those most often performed in 1790 were three works composed and first staged in Vienna during Joseph's reign: Paisiello's *Il re Teodoro in Venezia*, Martín's *L'arbore di Diana*, and Mozart's *Le nozze di Figaro*.[8] But the operatic climate changed quite suddenly in 1791, as Leopold took personal control of the direction of the Burgtheater and embarked on an ambitious and radical transformation of both personnel and repertory.

Having spent all his adult life in Italy, Leopold had theatrical tastes very different from those prevalent in Vienna. *Opera seria* was an essential element of operatic repertory in Florence, as elsewhere in Italy: an average of just under four *opere serie* were performed each year in Florence during the 1780s. Leopold set out to make the genre an essential element of Viennese theater as well.[9] In addition to organizing a new ballet troupe, dismissing the librettist Lorenzo Da Ponte and the soprano Adriana Ferrarese (the first Fiordiligi) and replacing them with a poet and a soprano whose ideas about *opera buffa* were closer to Leopold's own, the emperor assembled an *opera seria* troupe that included two of Italy's leading specialists in the genre: the soprano Cecilia Giuliani and the tenor Vincenzo Maffoli. On 27 July 1791, nineteen days after the contract for *La clemenza di Tito* was signed in Prague, Leopold sent a detailed memorandum to his music director, Count Wenzel Ugarte, specifying the operas in which his new *opera seria* singers were to make their Viennese debuts: *Teseo a Stige* by Sebastiano Nasolini (on the story of Phaedra and Hippolytus) and *La vendetta di Nino* by Alessio Prati (an operatic version of Voltaire's tragedy *Sémiramis*). Both operas had been first performed in Leopold's Florence; the emperor was almost certainly familiar with them.

Opera seria reached the stage of the Burgtheater on 24 November 1791, the birthday of Empress Maria Luisa, with a performance of *Teseo a Stige*. By scheduling the debut of his *opera seria* troupe on that particular day, Leopold returned to a practice followed by the Habsburg court earlier in the century, when many of Metastasio's dramas, including *La clemenza di Tito*, were first performed in celebration of the sovereigns' birthdays or namedays. Leopold's scheduling also suggests that Empress Maria Luisa as well as her husband favored the genre of *opera seria* and its re-establishment in Vienna.

The decision on the part of Governor Rottenhan and the Bohemian Estates to commission an *opera seria* for Leopold's coronation must have had its origins in the newly favored status of the genre in Vienna. Although Leopold's *opera seria* troupe had not yet made its debut when the coronation opera was commissioned on 8 July 1791, imperial approval of *opera seria* was already being signalled in late 1790 by Leopold's decision to employ Cecilia Giuliani; a contract with Vincenzo Maffoli in June 1791 confirmed that approval. It was only natural that the Bohemian nobility, many of whom had residences in Vienna and close connections to the court, and would have been aware of changes of taste at court, should respond to these changes with an *opera seria* of their own. Mozart's return to *opera seria* in 1791, after a decade in which he wrote no such operas, can be interpreted as an indirect result of the Habsburg court's return to this genre.

La clemenza di Tito as political allegory

Guardasoni's contract required that the coronation opera be a setting of a newly written libretto, or, if such a libretto could not be completed in time, that the opera be a setting of Metastasio's libretto *La clemenza di Tito*. Since time was so obviously short, this stipulation amounted to an agreement between Guardasoni and the Estates that Metastasio's libretto be set.

Metastasio's *La clemenza di Tito* was first performed in 1734, with music by the Habsburg court composer Antonio Caldara. During the period of thirty-eight years following the performance of Caldara's setting many of Europe's leading composers, including Hasse, Gluck, Wagenseil, Jommelli, Sarti, and Anfossi, set *La clemenza di Tito* to music. But between 1774 and 1791 not a single major composer is known with certainty to have set this libretto.[10] During the same period some of Metastasio's other librettos were set many times. (*L'Olimpiade* and *Antigono* received at least nine settings each; *Didone abbandonata* and *Alessandro nell'Indie* at least eight.)[11] Although highly respected as a work of literature, *La clemenza di Tito* was apparently not considered by leading composers to be suitable for the operatic stage during the two decades preceding Mozart's setting. Why then did Guardasoni and the Bohemian Estates single out *La clemenza di Tito* in 1791?

The libretto's political content must have been an important factor in the decision. At the height of the French Revolution Metastasio's drama showed the enlightened monarch being confronted with a violent rebellion and successfully suppressing it. At a time when revolutionary pamphlets were circulating scandalous stories about the incompetence and immorality of the crowned heads of Europe, the opera showed a ruler who was wise and virtuous; and it depicted the coup against him as both unnecessary and futile. Finally, and perhaps most important, an already established association between the Roman emperor Titus and the Habsburg monarch Leopold meant that the political allegory of *La clemenza di Tito* would be obvious both to the sovereign and to his subjects.

The eighteenth century saw theater as a potent shaper of political opinion and behavior. The views of the Italian playwright and librettist Giovanni De Gamerra, in a treatise called "Osservazioni sullo spettacolo," published in 1790, are typical:

True and wholesome theater reforms the heart, refreshes the spirit, and teaches us to live with circumspection. That is how theatrical spectacle becomes a school for the nation, where youth finishes its education with less danger than in social gatherings and clubs.

De Gamerra saw theater as an effective means for the sovereign to exercise his authority:

Theatrical spectacle, established on the basis of wise laws and of careful reform, can be regarded as a means always available to the sovereign power to inculcate in his subjects the most useful and important beliefs. In time of war it can increase patriotic heroism. In peace it can increase useful contacts among the people.

The theater is a school not only for the people but for the ruler as well, said De Gamerra, here citing one work in particular:

Has our century not seen an emperor at a performance of *La clemenza di Tito* listening to the voices of humanity and of forgiveness?[12]

Many eighteenth-century operas carried political messages; the political allegory of opera around the time of the French Revolution offers us a particularly vivid example of the connections between politics and theater. Consider some of the operas that reached the stage for the first time in 1791, as revolution continued to transform the political landscape of France and the rest of Europe looked on in alarm or admiration. In Paris audiences saw Grétry's *Guillaume Tell*, in which proud, virtuous Swiss citizens overthrew despotism (the opera was banned under Napoleon). Also in Paris, Cherubini's *Lodoiska* depicted the rescue of a virtuous woman from the clutches of a wicked tyrant. When Méhul's *Adrien* (libretto based on Metastasio's *Adriano in Siria*) was in rehearsal in Paris near the end of 1791 it caused a storm of protest from revolutionaries, who saw in the triumphal procession of Emperor Hadrian a favorable allusion to the Habsburg emperor Leopold. "The people of Paris would rather burn down the Opéra than see kings enjoy their triumph here." With these words the painter Jacques-Louis David is said to have joined others in keeping *Adrien* off the stage.[13]

The French saw their revolution mirrored and glorified on the stage; but another opera first performed in 1791 in a different part of Europe, *La clemenza di Tito*, showed revolution in a very different light.

Metastasio conceived *La clemenza di Tito* as a political libretto. Adam Wandruszka, biographer of Leopold II, has pointed out that the drama glorifies the idea of *clementia austriaca*, a tradition, long associated with the Habsburg dynasty, of enlightened rule, generous and lenient.[14] Metastasio's libretto was first performed to celebrate the birthday of Emperor Charles VI (Leopold's grandfather), and the title character was plainly meant to represent an idealized portrait of the Habsburg ruler. In a playful *licenza*, or epilogue, that Metastasio addressed to Charles and attached to the first edition of the libretto, the poet coyly protested that he did not intend the character of Tito to be a portrait of Charles, but his denial makes clear that the parallel was indeed intended:

Do not believe it, Sire. I did not try to portray you in Tito . . . I see well that everyone recognizes you in him; I know that you feel in your heart those generous emotions that Tito felt in his. But is it my fault, CAESAR, that others know this? Is it my fault that you resemble him? Ah, invincible AUGUSTUS, if you do not wish to admire images of yourself, forbid the muses to remember heroes.

The allegory of Metastasio's libretto is so general in its allusions that *La clemenza di Tito* could be performed in many parts of Europe during the eighteenth century, and in the presence of many different rulers. Yet a performance before Leopold in 1791 was particularly apt, not only because of the revolutionary political climate that prevailed at the time, but also because of the strong likelihood that audiences, including the emperor himself, would recognize Leopold in the character of Titus.

Titus, already remembered in antiquity as a model of the benevolent ruler, was compared with many modern rulers during the age of enlightened absolutism, both before and after Metastasio wrote his drama for Charles VI in 1734. But unusually strong associations developed, even before 1791, between Leopold and

Titus. Grand Duke Leopold's enlightened reign in Florence had caused several of his Tuscan subjects to compare him to Titus. In a guide to the collections of the Uffizi published in 1783 the author paused before a bust of Titus and thought immediately of Grand Duke Leopold, although he did not need to mention him by name: "Fortunate Tuscany," he wrote, "we have no need to envy Rome for the happy days of Titus." Poems published in the *Gazzetta toscana*, an official newsletter of the Tuscan court, made a habit of comparing the Grand Duke with Titus. "Both just and pious," wrote one poet to Leopold, "only you can surpass the memorable deeds of Antoninus and of Titus." After Joseph's death and Leopold's departure for Vienna, a poem expressed the Florentines' distress at having lost their ruler: "And if you, modern-day Titus, are not near, who will give us instruction and advice?"[15]

The same imagery was taken up in Germany. A Latin inscription erected by the Elector of Bohemia at Frankfurt during Leopold's imperial coronation imputed to Leopold various specific attributes of the Roman emperors. The attribute that Leopold shared with Titus, a year before *La clemenza di Tito* was performed in Prague, was clemency: "Celebrate, fortunate Germany. You have an emperor who is a Trajan in goodness, a Titus in clemency, and a [Marcus] Aurelius in wisdom. Now the golden age returns!"[16]

But it was left to one Joseph Sartori systematically to lay out the parallels between Leopold and Titus. *Leopoldinische Annalen* is a two-volume account, unremittingly favorable, of Leopold's reign; the second volume appeared in 1793, after Leopold's death. Towards the end of this volume Sartori compared the Roman emperor Titus to Leopold, whom he called "the German Titus."

[Leopold's] principal motto, "The hearts of his subjects are a ruler's greatest wealth," seemed to be an expression of his own heartfelt emotions. Rarely has a parallel been so appropriate as that between the character of Leopold and that of the Roman Titus. Both died in their forty-fifth year. Both ruled a little over two years ... All the virtues with which history has painted the portrait of the Roman Titus distinguished for us that of the German Titus. Fairness, benevolence, justice, charity were the characteristic features of both rulers. The warm wish of Titus to see all his subjects happy was disturbed by the rebellion of nature, in the form of earthquakes followed by plague and other natural disasters; rebellions of man disturbed Leopold's equally warm wishes. He had to subdue the rebellious Netherlands by force of arms. Immediately after peace was restored Leopold's exalted clemency declared a general amnesty for all those seduced and deluded [into rebellion]; just as Titus granted to patrician conspirators life and forgiveness. The patricians appreciated the clemency of Titus; a great part of the Netherlands did not appreciate the clemency granted to them by Leopold, and caused new anxiety to his kind, paternal heart. The Romans were far more grateful than the Christians of the enlightened eighteenth century.[17]

Sartori's exposition of the parallels between the Roman Titus and "the German Titus" leaves little doubt that attentive audiences of Mozart's opera made the same connection, even without being able to draw some of the parallels that Sartori did; they could not know, for example, that Leopold would soon die, so that his reign and his life were to be as short as those of Titus.

Having identified Leopold with the protagonist of the drama played before them, the audience could have easily recognized, in the violent and frightening coup with which Act I of *La clemenza di Tito* ends, the revolutionary movements that faced Leopold in 1791, just as Sartori drew a parallel between the patrician conspirators who threatened Titus and "the rebellious Netherlands" that threatened the peace of Leopold's reign.

Two important tasks were involved in turning Metastasio's old libretto into a modern opera rich in contemporary political associations. First it had to be revised. Then, of course, it had to be set to music. We shall see in the following chapters that the way in which both of these tasks were accomplished in 1791 had the effect of enhancing the libretto's allegorical content. Both revision and composition focussed the audience's attention on three of Metastasio's original six characters, and simplified the plot so that it revolved around the interactions of these three, thus making it easier to draw allegorical interpretations from the character and actions of the principals; they downplayed the more positive and inspiring aspects of the opera's revolutionary rhetoric; they emphasized the horror and violence, the senselessness and shame of revolution.

Mozart's Tito suppresses the rebellion, forgives the participants, and the opera ends with a chorus of praise for the virtuous, steadfast emperor. As Mozart's triumphant finale echoed through Prague's National Theater on the evening of Leopold's coronation day, the relevance of the opera to contemporary events must have been felt by many in the audience. To Leopold, "the German Titus," it implied that through *clemenza*, through generosity and forgiveness, he could win and keep the love of his subjects; to his subjects it warned that revolution would bring only destruction and shame – that allegiance to the virtuous Emperor-King Leopold, and to the system of government from which he derived his power, would bring an end to the crisis facing the Habsburg monarchy and a return to peace and prosperity.

2 *Metastasio the romantic*

The author of the libretto of *La clemenza di Tito* was born in Rome in 1698 and christened Antonio Trapassi. Gian Vincenzo Gravina, a wealthy Roman lawyer and man of letters, adopted Trapassi when he was ten years old and changed his name to Pietro Metastasio. Gravina was a founding member of the Arcadian Academy, a literary and intellectual organization that first met in 1690, and whose goal was the improvement of Italian poetry and drama. Growing up among the Arcadians, Metastasio absorbed their precepts: that clarity should be valued over complexity, that subtle wit and delicate sensibility should be valued over extravagance and bombast, that literature and drama should give pleasure as they lead their audience toward virtue and reason.

The Arcadians devoted much of their efforts to serious opera. Strongly influenced by French seventeenth-century moral philosophy (as articulated by Descartes, among others) and drama (Corneille and Racine), members of the Arcadian Academy and of similar academies in other Italian cities wrote librettos that banned the comic characters who had mingled with serious ones in many seventeenth-century Italian operas, carefully followed the Aristotelian unities and the *bienséances* of French classical tragedy, limited the use of spectacular scenic effects and emphasized refined craftsmanship and literary polish. The efforts of the Arcadians contributed much to the evolution of Italian opera during the late seventeenth and early eighteenth centuries.[1]

Although trained as a lawyer, Metastasio devoted his life to poetry, most of it in the form of librettos that embodied more successfully than those of any other poet the ideals of the Arcadian Academy. Between 1723 and 1771 he wrote twenty-seven three-act heroic librettos, or *drammi per musica*, works admired both for their literary value and for their effectiveness as musical theater. Composers, singers, and audiences alike recognized the excellence

16

of Metastasio's graceful and lively dramas: over the course of the eighteenth century composers made hundreds of settings of Metastasio's librettos, and he became recognized as one of the century's leading literary and theatrical figures.[2]

During the first years of his theatrical career Metastasio worked mainly in Naples and Rome; but in 1729 the Habsburg court called him to Vienna to replace Apostolo Zeno as court librettist. He went north the following year and remained in Vienna for the rest of his life, supplying the court with many of his finest *drammi per musica* as well as a wide variety of other kinds of theatrical poetry.

Metastasio brought together elements of early eighteenth-century Italian opera, Italian epic poetry of the sixteenth and seventeenth centuries, and French classical tragedy to create librettos of great beauty and strength. Like Corneille and Racine, Metastasio followed requirements of dramatic unity prescribed by – or, in some cases, wrongly ascribed to – Aristotle. Most of his dramas take place within a single day, in a single place; many of them can be said to be organized around a single great event. Metastasio usually respected the French rules of decorum, the *bienséances*, which kept off the stage passionate love-making, violent acts of any kind, and death, occurring naturally or otherwise. He followed French tragedy in believing that only noble and royal characters are dignified enough to feel, as Racine put it in his preface to *Bérénice*, "that majestic sadness that is the chief pleasure of tragedy."

Metastasio was fascinated by the intricacies of human emotion. His dramas follow with exquisite detail the conflicted feelings of men and women caught up in moral and emotional dilemmas. Much of Metastasio's tragedy is internal: he focussed interest on the struggles within his characters as well as between them. Following in the footsteps of Corneille and Racine, Metastasio often set up situations in which his characters have to decide between love and duty, between private interest and public good, a classic dilemma represented anagrammically AMOR/ROMA. The resolution of this dilemma often turns on an act of will by which a noble hero or heroine triumphs over the desire to give way to some merely personal feeling.

Conflict between characters and within characters: this dichotomy between external and internal struggle is reflected in the structure of Metastasio's librettos, their division into dialogue on the one hand and soliloquies and arias on the other. The dialogue is the realm of action. Here the dramatic situation is defined, the characters presented and developed; here the characters interact, much as they interact in a play by Corneille or Racine. The soliloquy and aria are the realms of feeling, analogous to the soliloquies of spoken drama. Here the characters express, with the help of music, their state of mind, their feelings, their internal conflicts.

The historical Titus

Like Corneille and Racine, Metastasio favored ancient history as a source for his dramas. He set *La clemenza di Tito* in a period of Roman history, the early empire, that was of special interest to both of his French predecessors. Metastasio took as his hero a ruler who had been the subject of plays by both Corneille and Racine, the Roman emperor Titus Flavius Vespasianus, who ruled from 79 to 81 A.D. (Plate 3).

Titus was born in 39 A.D., son of the powerful military commander Vespasian.[3] He spent his boyhood at the court of Emperor Claudius, where he was well trained in rhetoric as well as in military affairs. Having served in the army in Germany and Britain, Titus joined a legion under the command of his father in Palestine, where the Romans were involved in a war against the Jews. When Vespasian was declared emperor by his troops in 69, "the year of the four emperors," he left Titus in command in Palestine and went to Rome to claim the imperial throne. Titus captured Jerusalem in 70, after a long and difficult siege. His triumph was commemorated by the erection of an arch, magnificently decorated with reliefs, that still stands in Rome.

Titus joined his father, now in full control of the Empire, in Rome. As heir-apparent Titus's popularity was not great: his affair with the Jewish princess Berenice, daughter of King Herod Agrippa, contributed to his unpopularity, for the idea that a foreign princess should share the imperial throne was abhorrent to Romans. Titus demonstrated clear-headed political pragmatism as well as respect for public opinion and for Roman tradition by breaking off his relations with Berenice and sending her away. (This is the subject of Corneille's *Tite et Bérénice* and Racine's *Bérénice*, both performed in 1680.) He also dismissed some of his favorite boys (an action discreetly ignored by Corneille, Racine, and Metastasio).

3 Emperor Titus. Roman sculpture in marble, c. 80 A.D.

On Vespasian's death in 79 Titus began what came to be remembered as a wise and benevolent reign. He put an end to prosecution for treason and to the practice of relying on a network of informers to keep track of his subjects. Titus was a generous ruler, spending large sums on lavish entertainments for the populace and beautifying Rome with new buildings. He completed the great amphitheater that came to be known as the Colosseum. He contributed generously to the relief of Pompeii, destroyed in 79 by an eruption of Mount Vesuvius. Titus's reign was a period of peace throughout most of the Roman Empire, all too short a period: after ruling for little more than two years he died on 13 September 81.

The Roman historian Suetonius, who wrote his history of the first twelve emperors of Rome around 120 A.D., had much praise for Titus, who, he said, "had such winning ways ... that he became an object of universal love and adoration," *amor ac deliciae generis humani.* Suetonius's short account of Titus's reign is the most complete that survives from antiquity; it has been influential in shaping posterity's favorable view of Titus. But was Titus really as good as Suetonius portrays him? A recent study of Titus concluded that in many ways he deserved his reputation; but he was also a very clever politician who knew how to make the most of his good qualities. The warmness of Suetonius's account reflects both the emperor's deeds and his skillful manipulation of public opinion.[4]

Literary sources

The episode out of which Metastasio wove his drama is mentioned briefly by Suetonius:

Titus dismissed with a caution two patricians convicted of aspiring to the Empire; he told them that since this was a gift of Destiny they would be well advised to renounce their hopes. He also promised them whatever else they wanted, within reason, and hastily sent messengers to reassure the mother of one of the pair, who lived some distance away, that her son was safe. Then he invited them to dine among his friends; and, the next day, to sit close by him during the gladiatorial show, where he asked them to test the blades of the contestants' swords brought to him for inspection.[5]

When *La clemenza di Tito* was first published in 1734 Metastasio claimed in a statement affixed to his libretto that he based his drama on an episode in the life of the emperor Titus, and cited Suetonius and three other historians: Aurelius Victor, Dio Cassius and the Byzantine Zonaras. There is indeed some historical basis to the drama. Metastasio derived the character of Tito primarily from Suetonius's depiction, and he built the dramatic action around the attempted coup to which Suetonius refers. But beyond that, *La clemenza di Tito*, like many eighteenth-century librettos purporting to be based on historical events and characters, is mostly fiction. Metastasio provided Suetonius's two patricians with names: Sesto and Lentulo (the latter appears only briefly on stage near the end of the opera). He may have found the names of two other characters, Vitellia and Servilia, in an old libretto by Matteo Noris, *Tito Manlio* (the title role of which, however, is the consul Titus

Manlius, not the emperor Titus).[6] But Metastasio's most important source of inspiration was, as we might expect, French tragedy. He found the characters of Vitellia, the instigator of the rebellion, and of Sesto, who carries it out, in two of the most admired of French seventeenth-century tragedies, Corneille's *Cinna, ou la clémence d'Auguste* (1642) and Racine's *Andromaque* (1667). These dramas helped Metastasio not only with his title, but also with the general conduct of the plot, with the delineation of characters, and with individual turns of phrase.[7]

Metastasio's heroine–villain Vitellia, who seduces Sesto, a friend of the emperor, into rebellion, owes much both to Corneille's Emilie, in *Cinna*, and Racine's Hermione, in *Andromaque*. Beautiful Emilie, whose father was executed by order of Emperor Augustus, is full of hatred for the emperor and utterly ruthless; she persuades her lover Cinna, a friend of Augustus, to assassinate him. Cinna, protesting her harshness, calls Emilie a tyrant:

> Il faut sur un tyran porter de justes coups,
> Mais apprenez qu'Auguste est moins tyran que vous.
> > (*Cinna*, Act III, Sc. 4)

> A tyrant deserves to be attacked but you should know that Auguste is less of a tyrant than you.

A few lines later Cinna cries out against the power of Emilie's beauty:

> l'empire inhumain qu'exercent vos beautés

> the inhuman empire ruled by your beauty

Sesto, passionately in love with Vitellia, echoes Cinna:

> Oh sovrumano
> Poter della beltà! Voi, che dal cielo
> Tal dono aveste, ah! non prendete esempio
> Dalla tiranna mia. Regnate, è giusto:
> Ma non così severo,
> Ma non sia così duro il vostro impero.
> > (*La clemenza di Tito*, Act I, Sc. 4)[8]

> Oh superhuman power of beauty! You who have received this gift from heaven, ah, do not follow the example of my tyrant. Rule: that is just. But let your empire be less severe, less harsh than hers.

Racine's Hermione, like Emilie, uses the man in love with her to strike at a ruler. King Pyrrhus, with whom Hermione is in love, is about to marry Andromaque. Enraged with jealousy, Hermione persuades Oreste, who loves her, to murder Pyrrhus, promising Oreste that she will give herself to him if he does the deed:

> Revenez tout couvert du sang de l'infidèle;
> Allez: en cet état soyez sûr de mon cœur.
>
> (*Andromaque*, Act IV, Sc. 3)

> Come back all covered with the traitor's blood; go: thus you will be certain of my heart.

Metastasio's Vitellia is just as vivid in her bloody promise to Sesto:

> Ritorna asperso
> Di quel perfido sangue; e tu sarai
> La delizia, l'amore,
> La tenerezza mia. (*La clemenza di Tito*, Act I, Sc. 11)

> Return soaked in that perfidious blood; and you will be my delight, my love, my tenderness.

Oreste does what Hermione commands: he murders King Pyrrhus. But when he returns to Hermione with the news, she explodes with rage and grief before her astonished suitor:

HERMIONE
> Tais-toi, perfide,
> Et n'impute qu'à toi ton lâche parricide.
> Va, faire chez tes Grecs admirer ta fureur,
> Va, je la désavoue, et tu me fais horreur.
> Barbare, qu'as-tu fait? Avec quelle furie
> As-tu tranché le cours d'une si belle vie?
> Avez-vous pu, cruels, l'immoler aujourd'hui,
> Sans que tout votre sang se soulevât pour lui?
> Mais parle: de son sort qui t'a rendu l'arbitre?
> Pourquoi l'assassiner? Qu'a-t-il fait? A quel titre?
> Qui te l'a dit?

ORESTE
> O Dieux! Quoi? ne m'avez-vous pas
> Vous-même, ici, tantôt, ordonné son trépas?

HERMIONE
> Ah! fallait-il en croire une amante insensée?
> Ne devais-tu pas lire au fond de ma pensée?
> Et ne voyais-tu pas, dans mes emportements,
> Que mon coeur démentait ma bouche à tous moments?
>
> (*Andromaque*, Act V, Sc. 3)

HERMIONE
> Silence, wretch, and blame this wicked parricide on no one but yourself. Go back to your Greeks and let them admire your fury. Go, I disown you; you horrify me. What have you done,

barbarian? What fury made you cut off in its prime a life so beautiful? Could you and your cruel accomplices sacrifice him without your blood crying out for him? But speak. Who made you the judge of his fate? Why did you assassinate him? What did he do? By what right? Who told you to do it?

ORESTE

Gods! What? Did not you yourself order his death, here, a short time ago?

HERMIONE

Ah! how could you believe the ravings of a woman in love? Should you not have read my inmost thoughts? And did you not see in my distraction that my heart constantly belied my mouth?

In much the same way Vitellia reacts to Sesto's news that Tito is dead:

VITELLIA

        Orror mi fai. Dove si trova
Mostro peggior di te? Quando s'intese
Colpo più scellerato? Hai tolto al mondo
Quanto avea di più caro; hai tolto a Roma
Quanto avea di più grande. E chi ti fece
Arbitro de' suoi giorni?
Dì, qual colpa, inumano!
Punisti in lui? L'averti amato? È vero,
Questo è l'error di Tito;
Ma punir nol dovea chi l'ha punito.

SESTO

Onnipotenti dei! son io? Mi parla
Così Vitellia? E tu non fosti . . .

VITELLIA

            Ah! Taci,
Barbaro, e del tuo fallo
Non volermi accusar. Dove apprendesti
A secondar le furie
D'un'amante sdegnata? (*La clemenza di Tito*, Act II, Sc. 6)

VITELLIA

You horrify me. Where can there be a more hideous monster than you? When has there been a deed more wicked? You have taken from the world its most treasured possession; you have taken from Rome its greatest attribute. Who made you the judge of his fate? Tell me, cruel man, what was his fault that you punished? That he loved you? It is true: that was Tito's mistake; but he had no need to punish the man who punished him.

SESTO

Almighty gods! Am I awake? Is Vitellia speaking thus to me? And did you not . . .

VITELLIA

Ah! Silence, barbarian, and do not try to accuse me of your wickedness. Where did you learn to follow the ravings of a woman scorned in love?

Metastasio's Tito is partly modelled on Corneille's Auguste, a reluctant ruler, uncomfortable with the responsibilities and uncertainties of imperial power:

> J'ai souhaité l'empire, et j'y suis parvenu,
> Mais en le souhaitant, je ne l'ai pas connu,
> Dans sa possession j'ai trouvé pour tous charmes
> D'effroyables soucis, d'éternelles alarmes,
> Mille ennemis secrets, la mort à tous propos,
> Point de plaisir sans trouble, et jamais de repos.
>
> (*Cinna*, Act II, Sc. 1)

> I hoped for the empire, and I attained it, but in hoping for it I did not know it; now that I have it I have found, for all its charms, frightful cares, never ending alarms, a thousand secret enemies, death at every turn, no pleasure without trouble, and never rest.

Tito expresses similar complaints. In his first aria he says that the opportunity to do good is the only satisfaction that he has as ruler:

> Del più sublime soglio
> L'unico frutto è questo:
> Tutto è tormento il resto,
> E tutto è servitù. (*La clemenza di Tito*, Act I, Sc. 5)

> This is the only reward of the highest throne: all the rest is torment, all the rest is servitude.

And in his second aria Tito uses the word *tormento* again to refer to the cares of his reign:

> Ah! se fosse intorno al trono
> Ogni cor così sincero,
> Non tormento un vasto impero,
> Ma saria felicità. (*La clemenza di Tito*, Act I, Sc. 9)

> If everyone who approached the throne were this sincere, a vast empire would be not torment but happiness.

When Tito faces Sesto alone in their climactic confrontation in Metastasio's final act, Tito asks Sesto what he hoped to accomplish by assassinating him:

> E che sperasti
> Di trovar mai nel trono? Il sommo forse
> D'ogni contento? Ah! sconsigliato! Osserva
> Quai frutti io ne raccolgo;
> E bramalo, se puoi. (*La clemenza di Tito*, Act III, Sc. 6)

> And whatever did you hope to find on the throne? Supreme
> happiness, perhaps? How foolish you are! Look at the rewards I
> receive from it; and envy them, if you can.

Metastasio derived the idea of Tito's clemency in part from
Suetonius's account of Titus, and in part from Corneille's Auguste,
who generously pardons those who have plotted against him, but
only after a struggle with his own emotions. Auguste expresses the
triumph of his clemency in these memorable lines; his is a triumph
not over Cinna, but over himself:

> Je suis maître de moi comme de l'univers;
> Je le suis; je veux l'être. O siècles, o mémoire,
> Conservez à jamais ma dernière victoire! (*Cinna*, Act V, Sc. 3)

> I am master of myself as of the world: I am; I wish to be. Oh
> centuries, oh posterity, preserve my last victory for ever!

The words with which Auguste pronounces his pardon, the last line
of Corneille's play,

> Auguste a tout appris, et veut tout oublier (*Cinna*, Act V, Sc. 3)

> Auguste has learned all, and wishes to forget all

provided Metastasio with a model for the pronouncement of
forgiveness by his even more clement Tito:

> Sia noto a Roma
> Ch'io son l'istesso, e ch'io
> Tutto so, tutti assolvo, e tutto obblio.
> (*La clemenza di Tito*, Act III, Sc. 13)

> Let it be known to Rome that I have not changed: that I know all,
> forgive all, and forget all.

Tracing the idea of clemency further back, we find that a
principal source of inspiration for Corneille was *De clementia*, a
treatise by Seneca, the Roman philosopher, playwright, and
teacher of the emperor Nero. In Book I, chapter 9 of *De clementia*,
Seneca tells the story of Cinna's assassination attempt and Augustus's clemency. Corneille translated verbatim much of this
account and set it in his play. Metastasio, in borrowing so much

material from French seventeenth-century drama, was clearly following the example set by the French dramatists themselves, paying the same compliment to Corneille and Racine that Corneille had paid to Seneca and that Racine, in *Andromaque*, had paid to Virgil and Euripides.

Metastasio's Tito, for all his beneficence, is not a particularly happy ruler; Racine's *Bérénice*, which takes as its subject the parting of Titus and the Jewish princess Berenice, can help us to understand why this is so. Although they are deeply in love Titus puts his duties as ruler of Rome first, denying himself the source of his greatest satisfaction and pleasure, his love for Berenice and hers for him. Titus is in despair; he cries out:

> Ah Rome! Ah Bérénice! Ah prince malheureux!
> Pourquoi suis-je empereur? Pourquoi suis-je amoureux?
>
> (*Bérénice*, Act IV, Sc. 6)

> Ah, Rome! Ah, Berenice! Ah, wretched prince! Why am I emperor? Why am I in love?

Titus and Berenice part at the end of Racine's drama. Her departure from Rome is referred to near the beginning of Metastasio's *La clemenza di Tito* as having just happened. Since both Racine and Metastasio follow the classical precept of unity of time, we can conclude that Metastasio's drama takes place on the day following that on which Racine's drama takes place. This would explain much of Tito's resignation, the lack of pleasure that he feels in his reign. This would explain too why Metastasio's Tito lacks the passion of Racine's Titus: he has just given up the only thing that aroused his passion. We must think of Tito as a man who has sacrificed much and suffered much. His clemency, his generosity: these are the only things of value that Tito has left.

Convention and theatricality in *La clemenza di Tito*

In Metastasio's *La clemenza di Tito* one can see many of the features typical of his approach to the *dramma per musica*, which he helped to develop into a highly stylized, conventionalized theatrical genre. There are six characters. Most of Metastasio's librettos have six or seven characters, including a ruler (normally assigned to a tenor by eighteenth-century composers), a young prince or nobleman (normally assigned to a *musico*) in love with a beautiful princess or noblewoman (female soprano). In *Tito* the ruler is Tito himself, the young nobleman is Sesto, and the woman with whom he is in love is Vitellia.

Metastasio's libretto is in three acts. Like all of his *drammi per musica* it consists mostly of dialogue in blank verse, arranged in lines of seven or eleven syllables. This blank verse was meant to be declaimed by singers in a musical language of conventional melodic formulae, over an equally conventional harmonic foundation supplied by a keyboard instrument and often reinforced by a bass instrument, normally a cello. This conventional musical language was known in the eighteenth century as *recitativo semplice*, "simple recitative."

The unfolding of the drama in simple recitative is punctuated from time to time by arias, usually sung by a character just before leaving the stage (hence the term "exit-aria"). The arias are in a variety of poetic meters with various rhyme schemes. Most consist of two stanzas of four lines each. Metastasio conceived most of these two-stanza poems for a particular aria-form, the da capo aria, in which the setting of the first stanza is repeated after the setting of the second stanza.

Ensembles are rare in Metastasio's dramas, choruses normally even rarer. *La clemenza di Tito* has no ensembles; it has two choruses, the second of which is performed twice as a way of framing the final scene.

Judging Metastasian music-drama from the point of view of dramaturgical and musical conventions that are irrelevant to it has led to misunderstanding of *opera seria* in general and of Mozart's *La clemenza di Tito* in particular. Crucial to this misunderstanding is the idea that the blank verse, the dialogue in simple recitative, is of less importance dramatically than the arias because it is less interesting than the arias from a musical point of view. The problem is partly one of terminology. In the nineteenth century, after composers had stopped writing simple recitative, another term, derogatory by implication, came into common use: "secco recitative." The word *secco*, "dry," implies dullness, boredom. Many nineteenth- and twentieth-century critics have found it difficult to make sense of the long passages of "dry" recitative in eighteenth-century opera. Their inability to understand such "dry" recitative as anything but dull was in part a product of the anachronistic term with which they referred to it. Few critics went beyond their distaste for simple recitative to ask why composers used this particular musical technique to set blank verse.

One particularly vehement attack on *opera seria* may serve as an example. Robert Freeman's study of Antonio Caldara's settings of librettos by Zeno and Metastasio brought to its subject the assumption, implicit in much modern operatic criticism, that an opera is dramatic only insofar as the music mirrors and enhances the emotions and dramatic situations represented on stage.[9] Freeman's ideal of baroque opera was Monteverdi's richly expressive monody. He searched Caldara's simple recitative for signs of the composer responding to words, emotions and dramatic situations with imaginative and expressive musical gestures. He looked in vain, and criticized librettist and composer for not coming up to the standards of early baroque opera: ". . . neither Zeno nor Caldara had ever had the fortune to experience a Monteverdi opera."[10]

Freeman reported with disappointment that "*secco* recitative hardly ever makes very interesting reading." This is hardly surprising; simple recitative was not meant to be read. It was meant to be declaimed on the stage by skillful and energetic singer-actors. But more important, Freeman missed the point of simple recitative by concentrating on the music rather than the words. He called Caldara's work "opera without drama" because he was looking for drama in the wrong place. Much of *opera seria*'s substance – much of its emotion, its beauty and meaning – lies in the blank verse. But here the text was meant to be of much greater interest than the music. One should not expect the musical highpoints of the drama necessarily to coincide with or to reinforce all the dramatic highpoints, as they do in many other kinds of opera. Often exactly the opposite is true. The musical spareness and conventionality of simple recitative was meant to focus the listener's attention on the words, on the action.

The English essayist and novelist Vernon Lee (pseudonym of Violet Paget, 1856–1935) worked to counteract the tendency of nineteenth-century critics to dismiss Metastasio's librettos and musical settings of them as undramatic. Lee's discussion of Metastasian dramaturgy in *Studies of Italy in the eighteenth century*, first published in 1880, is extraordinary in its sensitivity to the value of Metastasio's blank verse and its understanding of the dramatic and musical context in which the blank verse should be considered:

As the opera was an artistic form, distinct and different from tragedy, so also Metastasio was a different sort of poet from Shakespeare and Lope de Vega, from Corneille and Racine; as the opera was a combination of two very distinct musical forms, recitative and air, so also Metastasio was a poet of two very distinct categories: a dramatist and a lyrist . . . The opera, in its duality, belonged half to the poet, half to the musician; they were subservient to each other by turns: in the recitative, the musician, composer, and singer helped the poet, worked to give his verse the strongest, most artistic expression; in the air, the poet helped the musician, laboured to give him, composer and singer, the greatest scope of free melodic invention and execution. The notes of Pergolesi, the intonations of Farinello, were of first-rate beauty in the recitative, but its real absorbing interest was the words of Metastasio; in the airs the rhymes of Metastasio were often of first-rate beauty, but the real, absorbing interest was the melodies and harmonies of Pergolesi, the swells, and runs, and shakes of Farinello.[11]

Once we take Metastasio's blank verse as the core of his drama, and stop thinking of it as dull, dry recitative that should be cut so that we can hear the next aria as soon as possible, its theatricality begins to reveal itself, and its musical simplicity beings to make dramatic sense. Only then can we appreciate "Metastasio's aim and his glory," as Lee put it: "To conceive an emotional situation, to develop it, gradually yet swiftly, marking each step, each movement, even as a musician would develop a theme . . ." Lee evokes the spirit of Metastasio's dramas with reference to *La clemenza di Tito*:

To obtain opportunities for such development was his constant thought; he was for ever seeking for pathetic situations, he loved to crowd them together. The subjects treated by the ancients and by the French did not satisfy him, they were too meagre for him. He would take the main situations from a half a dozen plays and poems, and work them into one plot, combining together in his *Titus* the *Cinna* of Corneille and the *Andromaque* of Racine; weaving together Sophocles and La Motte, Ariosto and Racine, Lope and Herodotus, and then, in the prose argument prefixed to his play, referring the reader with grand vagueness to Strabo, Pliny, Sanchoniathon, any one; as romantic as Shakespeare or Calderon, while thinking he was correct and classic as Maffei.[12]

This idea of Metastasio as "romantic" is one of Lee's most important contributions to our understanding of eighteenth-century *opera seria*. It is a concept that she closely associated with the musical life of the period. More familiar than many more recent critics with the details of the production of eighteenth-century opera, Lee realized that when Metastasio's dramas are considered in the context of the theater of his time, they take on a character completely different from what one might expect from reading them on the printed page. Only when we understand eighteenth-century operatic life, suggested Lee in a passage that is one of her most brilliant and original, can we appreciate Metastasio's dramas, since they were shaped by that musical life:

Under the influence of composers and singers Metastasio received the finishing touches requisite to make him a romantic poet: it was impossible to conceive correct tragic folk, solemn Greeks and Romans like those of Corneille, Racine, Maffei, and Alfieri, in the midst of this strange and motley vocal world of the eighteenth century: of these women dressed as men, and boys dressed as women, in powder, velvet, rose-coloured doublets, hoops, jewelled helmets, immense feathers, many-buttoned gloves, and every eccentricity of cut and colour; of the soprano and contralto heroes and heroines, quarrelling and making love in richly modulated recitative, with fiddles to mark the cadence and hautboys to play the ritornellos, sighing their passion or threatening their anger in magnificently melodious airs with fugued accompaniments, or in won-drously subtle and flimsy woofs of swells and runs and curling turns and luminous shakes. A distinct race of beings, as distinct as the euphuistic, fantastically dainty young men and girls of Shakespeare, as distinct as the grotesquely wonderful masks and Kings of Hearts of Gozzi, was neces-sarily created under the influence of the proud, beautiful music of the Hasses, Leos, Pergolesis, and Jommellis.[13]

Many scholars since Lee have urged reappraisal of eighteenth-century *opera seria*, although none have done so more eloquently than she. The genre has recently begun to win acceptance among relatively large numbers of singers, conductors, opera directors and music-lovers. Mozart's setting of *La clemenza di Tito* has been one of the operas that has benefitted most from this gradual shift in opinion, as we shall see in chapter 8.

3 *Mazzolà's revision*

Metastasio wrote *La clemenza di Tito* for a particular occasion, with particular singers and a particular composer in mind. Like all eighteenth-century librettists, he knew that his dramas, when they were re-used under different circumstances, would have to undergo revisions. Throughout the eighteenth century Metastasio's librettos served as the basis for hundreds of operas; but rarely were they set as Metastasio wrote them. That Mozart's *La clemenza di Tito* uses a revision of Metastasio's libretto rather than Metastasio's original is not in itself remarkable; it puts the opera in the mainstream of settings of Metastasio's texts. When, in the summer of 1791, Caterino Mazzolà revised *La clemenza di Tito* for the coronation of Leopold II as King of Bohemia, he joined a long list of poets, most of whose names are unknown to us, who had revised this libretto for a wide variety of musical settings.[1]

Caterino Mazzolà

The career of Caterino Mazzolà (1745–1806) was in some ways similar to that of Mozart's previous Italian literary collaborator, Lorenzo Da Ponte.[2] Both began their literary careers in Venice; both specialized in comic opera. Mazzolà began writing librettos for the Venetian theaters in the late 1760s; one of his biggest early successes was *La scuola de' gelosi*, set to music by Salieri for the Venetian Carnival of 1779 and performed throughout Europe during the next two decades. Mazzolà and Da Ponte went north at about the same time, the former to Dresden, where he became court poet in 1780, the latter to Vienna. Da Ponte began his work as a librettist later than Mazzolà; his was still a "virgin muse" (a phrase he attributed to Joseph II) when the emperor employed him as theatrical poet, probably in 1783. Mazzolà had recommended Da Ponte to his former collaborator Salieri, and since Salieri was

31

Joseph's favorite composer this recommendation undoubtedly helped Da Ponte to win his job in Vienna.

Mazzolà's connection with Salieri was probably renewed in the spring of 1791, when Da Ponte was dismissed from the court theater by Joseph's successor, Leopold II. Mazzolà served as court librettist in Vienna from May to August 1791, when he was replaced in turn by yet another Venetian specialist in comic opera, Giovanni Bertati.[3]

We do not know who brought Mazzolà into the team that created *La clemenza di Tito*. It could have been Guardasoni; it could have been Mozart. It was presumably above all Mazzolà's presence in Vienna during the summer of 1791 that led to his collaboration with Mozart in *La clemenza di Tito*. Time was short; it would have been too late to bring a poet from Italy. Da Ponte, who could probably have done as good a job as Mazzolà, had already left Vienna in disgrace.

Mazzolà certainly was not chosen to revise Metastasio's libretto on account of any special experience in serious opera. Like Mozart, Mazzolà returned in *La clemenza di Tito* to a genre to which he had given little attention during the previous decade. Mazzolà had written his most recent serious librettos, *Elisa* and *Osiride*, in 1781, the year in which Mozart had completed his previous serious opera, *Idomeneo*. During the 1780s Dresden, in many ways a cultural satellite of Vienna, followed the Habsburg capital in preferring *opera buffa* to *opera seria*. From 1781 to 1791 Mazzolà, like Da Ponte, wrote no serious librettos; instead he supplied the Dresden composers Naumann, Seydelmann and Schuster with a series of at least thirteen comic works. When he turned suddenly back to serious opera in 1791, he brought with him much of what he had learned as a librettist of comic opera, as we shall see.

Conventional aspects of the *Tito* revision

Mazzolà's revision of *La clemenza di Tito* can best be understood in the context of the many revisions of Metastasio's librettos that were made in Italy during the late eighteenth century. The Italian musicologist Sergio Durante has laid out with impressive clarity the main procedures involved in these revisions.[4] Metastasio's librettos were almost always shortened by his revisers, who normally accomplished this by cutting recitative and reducing the number of arias. This abridgment allowed them often to compress the drama from the normal Metastasian three acts to two. Secondary characters, each carefully drawn by Metastasio, suffered especially from these cuts.

Durante cites as an example a revision of Metastasio's *Didone abbandonata* as performed in Florence in 1786 (a production, incidentally, in which Domenico Bedini, who was later to create the role of Sesto in Mozart's *La clemenza di Tito*, sang the role of Aeneas). One result of the shortening of that libretto from three acts to two was the reduction in dramatic importance of the three lesser roles, those of Selene, Araspe, and Osmida. Durante focusses on the role of Selene, Dido's sister, who is secretly in love with Aeneas. This character was invented by Metastasio, who developed it fully and wove it into his rich fabric of interconnecting plot-lines and characterizations. Selene's sweet, gentle personality represents a counterpoint to Dido's more demonstrative passion. The dilemma that Selene faces, between her love for Aeneas and her faithfulness to her sister and queen, represents one facet of the conflict between love and duty that lies at the heart of Metastasio's drama. But the anonymous poet who revised *Didone abbandonata* for Florence clearly saw Selene's part as irrelevant to the central theme of the opera: the love, jealousy and duty that bring Dido, Aeneas and Iarbas into conflict. The revision resulted in a simplification, a streamlining of the libretto's dramatic structure that emphasizes the principal plot-line and reduces Selene's role to that of a supporting character, Dido's confidante, with little emotion or initiative of her own.

The changes that Mazzolà made in *La clemenza di Tito* can be divided into two categories. In the first category are the changes that were made on almost any occasion when one of Metastasio's librettos was set to music in the 1780s and 1790s, changes that did not involve a departure from one of the fundamental principles of Metastasian music-drama: that the plot and the interaction between the characters be carried forward mainly by means of blank verse declaimed in simple recitative. In the other category is a more radical change, one that contradicted this basic tenet of Metastasian dramaturgy. The most noticeable changes in the first category are cuts in dialogue and the elimination or replacement of arias. In the second category is Mazzolà's transformation of Metastasio's dialogue in blank verse into ensembles.

A typical example of Mazzolà's many cuts is to be found in Act I, Scene 1, where the poet reduced the opening dialogue for Sesto and Vitellia by almost half, from ninety-eight lines of verse to fifty-four. He made a more extensive cut in Metastasio's Act II, eliminating a whole sequence of scenes, including four arias. He thereby excised one whole episode, in which Sesto's friend Annio, having exchanged cloaks with Sesto, is wrongly accused of having attempted to kill the emperor. With cuts like these, Mazzolà made his version of the libretto shorter and simpler than Metastasio's and was able to compress it into two acts.

Mazzolà performed his surgery carefully, limiting many of his cuts to scenes involving the three secondary roles (Annio, Annio's beloved Servilia, and the praetorian prefect Publio), attempting not to impair Metastasio's delineation of character and motivation in the three principal roles, and showing respect for the riches of Metastasio's blank verse. Mazzolà left many passages of blank verse almost completely untouched, including the great dialogue between Tito and Sesto in Metastasio's Act III (Mazzolà's Act II), in which Tito tries in vain to persuade Sesto to explain his motives for betraying his friend and sovereign.

It was a common procedure in arranging a libretto to replace original aria-texts with new texts. The libretto that Mozart set has three replacement aria-texts, all in what had been Metastasio's Act III, and one aria-text added where there was none in Metastasio's original. Mazzolà replaced Annio's aria "Pietà, signor, di lui" with "Tu fosti tradito," Sesto's "Vo disperato a morte" with "Deh per questo istante solo," and Vitellia's "Getta il nocchier talora" with "Non più di fiori"; he gave Annio a completely new aria, "Torna di Tito al lato."

One reason for replacing Metastasio's aria-texts was that new kinds of arias had been invented since Metastasio wrote his libretto. Few, if any, composers were still writing da capo arias in 1791; while they could, and often did, use Metastasio's two-stanza aria-texts for arias with more modern forms, they also needed texts specially written for modern aria-forms. This was the case, for example, with the two-tempo rondò. This type of aria, developed in the 1770s and still very popular in the 1790s, normally demanded a twelve-line poem in three stanzas, the lines consisting of seven or eight syllables each. Since the rondò did not exist when Metastasio wrote *La clemenza di Tito*, it is not surprising that his libretto contains no poem that could be set as a rondò. Nor is it surprising that two of the three replacement arias, "Deh per questo istante solo" and "Non più di fiori," are rondò-texts.

Mazzolà's ensembles

Careful pruning of Metastasio's libretto, the replacement of some of his aria-texts, and the reduction to two acts: none of these changes would have been considered unusual by the other poets revising Metastasio's librettos for productions in Italy during the 1780s and 1790s. But in one of his changes Mazzolà went well beyond most Italian revisions: he incorporated into Metastasio's libretto no fewer than eight ensembles.

Metastasio had nothing against ensembles. Most of his librettos have one or more; his *La clemenza di Tito* is atypical in its complete avoidance of them. But the number of Mazzolà's ensembles is exceptional, even by the standards of late eighteenth-century revisions of Metastasio's librettos: three duets, three trios, a quintet with chorus, and a sextet with chorus. Furthermore, many of these are what we might call "action-ensembles" – ensembles in which action takes place, in which the plot, with all its passion, uncertainty, and conflict, moves forward, and in which the relations between characters develop. Action-ensembles were foreign to Metastasio's approach to opera, for they took over the role that Metastasio assigned to blank verse and simple recitative.

Mazzolà's opening scene provides us with a good example of how he transformed Metastasio's libretto by replacing part of Metastasio's blank verse with action-ensembles. Metastasio conceived the opening scene, a long and richly detailed debate between Vitellia and Sesto, entirely in simple recitative: he provided for it ninety-eight lines of finely crafted blank verse. The scene ends with Sesto's promise that he will do whatever Vitellia commands. She orders him to assassinate Tito before sunset.

Although Mazzolà greatly shortened Metastasio's dialogue, he saw the necessity for preserving much of Metastasio's opening scene to establish the background of the plot and to delineate the characters of Vitellia and Sesto. More radical than this cutting of simple recitative is what Mazzolà did with the end of Metastasio's dialogue. He used the last five lines of blank verse as the basis for a duet between Vitellia and Sesto. He tried to preserve as much of Metastasio's blank verse as possible in the rhyming poetry of the duet; Metastasio's words are indicated below by the use of italics. But at the point where Metastasio's dialogue breaks off, Mazzolà's duet continues to an emotional climax that has no counterpart in Metastasio's libretto.

SESTO

Come ti piace *imponi*:
Regola i moti miei.
Il mio destin tu sei;
Tutto farò per te.

VITELLIA

Prima che il sol tramonti,
Estinto io vò l'indegno.
Sai ch'egli usurpa un regno,
Che in sorte il ciel mi diè.

SESTO

Già il tuo furor m'accende.

VITELLIA

Ebben, che più s'attende?

SESTO

Un dolce sguardo almeno
Sia premio alla mia fè!

VITELLIA e SESTO

Fan mille affetti insieme
Battaglia in me spietata.
Un'alma lacerata
Più della mia non v'è. (Mazzolà, Act I, Sc. 1)

SESTO

Command me as you like; control my every move. You are my destiny; I will do everything for you.

VITELLIA

Before the sun sets I want the wretch dead. You know he usurps a kingdom that heaven granted me by fate.

SESTO

Your fury already sets me aflame.

VITELLIA

Then what more are you waiting for?

SESTO

Let one sweet look at least be the reward for my devotion!

VITELLIA and SESTO

A thousand different feelings battle within me. There is no soul more tormented than mine.

Another ensemble to which Mazzolà transferred the interaction of characters that Metastasio had developed in blank verse is the trio "Vengo . . . Aspettate . . . Sesto!" sung by Vitellia, Annio, and Publio. Mazzolà formed this trio out of the blank verse of Metastasio's Act I, Scenes 12 and 13, in which Publio announces to Vitellia, after she has just sent Sesto off to start the rebellion, that Tito has chosen her to be his wife. Vitellia is thrown into panic by this turn of events. She expresses her confusion in recitative: first rapid-fire dialogue with Publio, then a passionate soliloquy, and finally she brings Act I to an end with an aria, "Quando sarà quel dì."

Mazzolà eliminated the aria and transformed the recitative into a trio in which Publio and Annio (whom he brought into the scene) add an ironic undercurrent by expressing, in an aside, the belief that Vitellia's confusion is the product of her joy at being chosen by Tito. As in the previous example, much of what Vitellia sings Mazzolà took from Metastasio's recitative (Metastasio's words are in italics below):

VITELLIA

> Vengo ... *aspetta*te ... *Sesto*! ...
> Ahimè! ... *Sesto*! ... *è partito*?
> Oh *sdegno* mio *funesto*!
> Oh insano mio furor!
> Che *angustia*, che tormento!
> Io *gelo*, oh Dio! d'orror.

PUBLIO e ANNIO

> *Oh come un gran contento,*
> *Come confonde* un cor. (Mazzolà, Act I, Sc. 10)

VITELLIA

> I'm coming ... wait ... Sesto! ... Oh no! ... Sesto! ... has he left? Oh my fatal anger! Oh my insane fury! What anguish, what torment! Oh God! I freeze with horror.

PUBLIO and ANNIO

> Oh how a great joy confuses a heart.

Mazzolà performed his most remarkable transformation of blank verse to action-ensemble in dealing with Metastasio's treatment of the rebellion instigated by Vitellia, or, to put it more accurately, in dealing with the succession of conversations and arias that takes place during the rebellion; for the rebellion itself, in keeping with the *bienséances*, takes place completely off-stage in Metastasio's libretto and is referred to only briefly by the characters on stage.

Metastasio placed the rebellion at the beginning of his second act. In reducing Metastasio's libretto from three acts to two, Mazzolà shifted the rebellion to the end of Act I. The rebellion suggested itself to Mazzolà as material out of which to develop a finale, an ensemble consisting of a sequence of connected musical sections, normally without any simple recitative, in which most, if not all, of an opera's characters come together in a dramatic climax at the end of an act.

This is exactly what Mazzolà made of the rebellion. He eliminated Metastasio's arias and transformed Metastasio's blank verse into an ensemble, using the same techniques that he used in his duets and trios. He added an important element not in Metastasio's libretto: the Roman populace, in the form of an off-stage chorus, cries out in horror at the events taking place, and those on stage react to the cries with shock and fear. Mazzolà brought on stage all the soloists except Tito, gradually building the number of singers on stage from one (Sesto, at the beginning of the finale), to five, at the end. The resulting quintet with chorus is a much longer, more elaborate text than those that Mazzolà provided for his duets and trios, bringing together different combinations of singers and a variety of emotional states. These were necessary ingredients in the text for a finale, for they encouraged the composer to create a musical setting with the changes of tempo, meter, and key that were expected in this kind of act-ending ensemble.

Aspects of *opera buffa* in Mazzolà's revision

La clemenza di Tito was by no means the first serious opera to use action-ensembles or finales. Johann Christian Bach experimented with such techniques in his setting of a libretto by Metastasio, *Temistocle*, as revised by the prolific and adventurous theatrical poet Mattia Verazi (Mannheim, 1772): Acts II and III of Bach's *Temistocle* end with finales. Giovanni Paisiello's *Pirro* (Naples, 1787) makes use not only of finales, but also of an *introduzione*, a finale-like ensemble at the beginning of the opera, and, like the finale, first used in comic opera.[5] Mazzolà's revision may well owe something to examples like these. But a much more obvious source of inspiration for Mazzolà was *opera buffa*, as Alfred Einstein implied in his discussion of Mazzolà's revision:

This libretto has the form, but of course not the spirit, of an *opera buffa*. It has two acts like an *opera buffa*, and the end of the first act is planned exactly on the principle of an *opera buffa*, that is, leaving the action quite up in the air, and the issue quite undecided. There are ensembles instead of arias, rapid progress in the action, and the expression of conflicting feelings in the ensembles.[6]

The idea that an opera's action and the feelings of its characters should be reinforced musically through the use of ensembles and finales was just as crucial a characteristic of late eighteenth-century *opera buffa* as it was foreign to Metastasian *opera seria*.

An indication that Mazzolà was thinking of *opera buffa* as he prepared his ensembles is his use, at least once, of material from one of his comic librettos. The following lines recur several times, like a refrain, in the ensemble-with-chorus with which Mazzolà brought to a close *La dama soldato* (set by Johann Gottlieb Naumann in Dresden, and performed during Spring 1791), the last libretto completed by Mazzolà before he set to work revising *Tito*:

> Quando un'alma è all'altra unita,
> Qual piacer un cor risente!
> Ah si tronchi dalla vita
> Tutto quel [che] non è amor.[7]

> When one soul is united with another, what pleasure fills the heart! Ah, let all that is not love be removed from life!

When Mazzolà wrote the duet for Annio and Servilia to sing in Act I of *La clemenza di Tito*, "Ah perdona al primo affetto," he based the first two quatrains on Metastasio's arias for Annio and Servilia. But for his final quatrain he had recourse to his own poetry: he reproduced the lines from *La dama soldato* word for word.[8] Poetry from a comic opera suddenly turning up in a serious one: what better illustration of the mixing of genres represented by Mazzolà's revision?

This mixing of the genres did great damage to Metastasio's original conception of the drama, as Vernon Lee pointed out amusingly, although she does not seem to have realized how atypical of late eighteenth-century revisions of Metastasio Mazzolà's was; nor did she mention how much of Metastasio's blank verse Mazzolà left intact.

Any one curious to see what a play by Metastasio had become by the year 1790 may compare *Clemenza di Tito* as printed in his works to *Clemenza di Tito* as set by Mozart: the powerful opening scene between Sextus and Vitellia is fiddle-faddled into a duet; the rapid scene of the discovered conspiracy is drawn out into a quintet [the first-act finale]; the pathetic meeting of Sextus and Titus is fugued and twisted into a trio, and the exquisite outburst of Sextus's remorse is frittered away into a long rondo, in which he repeats a dozen times and to all sorts of tunes – "Tanto affanno soffre un core – nè si muore – di dolore."[9]

However much it may have disappointed admirers of Metastasio's original libretto, it is not surprising that the incorporation of ensembles should have been attractive to Mazzolà, nor is it surprising that Mozart should have approved of it. Both poet and musician had been absorbed in the creation of comic opera during the 1780s. Italian opera in Vienna and, by extension, in Dresden, was comic opera. Even when Viennese operas incorporated much serious drama (as, for example, in Salieri's *Axur, re d'Ormus* and Mozart's *Don Giovanni*), they continued to follow the comic opera tradition of carrying much of the dramatic development forward in ensembles and finales.

By transforming Metastasio's blank verse into action-ensembles like the duet "Come ti piace imponi," the trio "Vengo ... aspettate ... Sesto! ..." and the finale of Act I, Mazzolà made it possible, indeed necessary, for the composer working with him to take part in the development of the characters and the relations between them, to a much greater extent than would have been allowed by Metastasio himself. Mozart, having grown used to such opportunities in the process of composing comic operas for Vienna and getting to know the dozens of comic operas by other composers performed in Vienna during the 1780s, welcomed them in Mazzolà's revision: when he entered *La clemenza di Tito* in his manuscript catalogue of his works, Mozart referred to the libretto with approval, describing it as having been *ridotta a vera opera* by Mazzolà, "reduced to true opera."

The politics of revision

Metastasio wrote his libretto at a time when there was little threat of revolution within the Habsburg realms. He was able to enliven his opera with some moving talk in favor of revolution, evidently without fear that it would attract the unwelcome attention of censors. Vitellia has some particularly strong language. Encouraging Sesto to undertake the rebellion, she refers to Brutus (either Lucius Junius Brutus, who led a rebellion against the last King of Rome in 509 B.C., or Marcus Junius Brutus, who took part in the plot to assassinate Julius Caesar in 44 B.C. in the hope of restoring the Roman republic):

> Io ti propongo
> La patria a liberar. Frangi i suoi ceppi;

La tua memoria onora;
Abbia il suo Bruto il secol nostro ancora.

(Metastasio, Act I, Sc. 11)

I propose to you that you liberate the fatherland. Break its
shackles; honor your own memory: let our century have its own
Brutus.

These last words would have sounded ambiguous and threatening
to a late eighteenth-century audience in the Habsburg monarchy. Is
"our century" the first century A.D., or is it the eighteenth? The
elder Brutus was one of the heroes of the French Revolution.
Voltaire's tragedy *Brutus*, performed in Paris in 1790, inflamed
revolutionary passions; David's painting of Brutus (1789) was also
appreciated for its revolutionary implications.[10] It is not surprising
that Mazzolà cut most of this passage (everything after "liberar"),
which must have sounded uncomfortably close to French revolutionary rhetoric. He also cut Vitellia's promise, quoted in
chapter 2 along with a similar passage in Racine's *Andromaque*,
that if Sesto should return to her soaked in Tito's blood he will
receive from her both love and pleasure. Even if Metastasio
modelled this passage on Racine, it is still remarkable for its vivid
imagery, its memorable juxtaposition of violence and the pleasant
reward for committing such violence; Mazzolà may well have
regarded it as unsuitable for a coronation opera.

Mazzolà's transformation of Metastasio's rebellion into his first-
act finale may also have political implications. In Metastasio's
libretto the coup takes place quickly, off-stage, and with apparently
little violence; it seems to be over almost as soon as it began. In
Mozart's opera the coup is staged more realistically; it is more
palpable and violent. As such, it could have been understood, by a
Habsburg monarch and his subjects seeing the opera performed in
1791, as a reference to the terrible events then taking place in
France, events that would lead, within less than three years, to the
execution of Louis XVI and of his wife – Emperor Leopold's sister
– Marie Antoinette.

Metastasio's rebellion is preceded by Sesto's monologue in which
he expresses his agony over the step he is about to take. After much
indecision he resolves finally not to carry out his treacherous plan,
but at that very moment the burning Capitol signals that the
rebellion has begun. Yet Sesto is still not certain that it is too late to
change his mind, even after seeing the fire. He still hopes to save
Tito's life, and goes off to try to do so:

> Forse già tardi
> Sono i rimorsi miei.
> Defendetemi Tito, eterni dei! (Metastasio, Act 2, Sc. 1)
>
> Perhaps my remorse has come too late. Eternal gods, defend Tito
> for me!

The rebellion in Mazzolà's revision is preceded by this same
monologue for Sesto. But once the rebellion begins, for Mozart's
Sesto there is no *forse*, no "perhaps." He not only sees the fire but
also hears the sound of clashing arms; Mazzolà added the lines

> Un gran tumulto io sento
> D'armi e d'armati (Mazzolà, Act I, Sc. 11)
>
> I hear a great tumult of arms and soldiers.

and Sesto ends the recitative with an unambiguous and painful cry,
likewise added by Mazzolà:

> Ahi! tardo è il pentimento.
>
> Ah! My repentence is too late.

In Metastasio's original the rebellion itself is described very
briefly by Publio, who announces that the Capitol is on fire. But the
fire still leaves room for doubt that it was lit on purpose, as Publio
says:

> Ah voglia il cielo
> Che un'opra sia del caso, e che non abbia
> Forse più reo disegno
> Chi destò quelle fiamme! (Metastasio, Act II, Sc. 4)
>
> Ah, would to heaven that this is the result of an accident, and that
> whoever set these flames had no criminal intent!

In Mazzolà's revision Publio has no doubt that the fire was
started on purpose, that a rebellion is in progress, and that Tito is in
danger; his words are more menacing:

> V'è in Roma una congiura,
> Per Tito, ahimè, pavento;
> Di questo tradimento
> Chi mai sarà l'autor? (Mazzolà, Act I, Sc. 12)
>
> There is a conspiracy in Rome, and fear for Tito's life. Who could
> be the instigator of this betrayal?

In Metastasio's drama Sesto announces to Vitellia that Tito has
been killed: he did not commit the deed, but he saw one of the

conspirators stab the emperor, in spite of his efforts to stop the deed. Sesto makes this declaration when he and Vitellia are alone on stage. Only they know of Tito's apparent death; and even they have some reason to doubt that he is dead, for Sesto uses the present tense in referring to the emperor's death:

> Già Tito ... Oh Dio! Già dal trafitto seno
> Versa l'anima grande. (Metastasio, Act II, Sc. 6)

> Already Tito ... Oh God! Already his great soul is flowing from his wounded breast.

Apparently Sesto did not wait for Tito to die; he only saw a man whom he thought was Tito fall; later it turns out that the man he saw being attacked was not in fact the emperor.

Mazzolà makes Sesto's actions more violent. Sesto's account is completely in the past tense; he seems to have no doubt that Tito is dead. Furthermore, his announcement is more public: not only Vitellia but Annio, Servilia, and Publio hear and react to the news that the emperor is dead. Sesto says nothing about having tried to save Tito's life; indeed he implies that he himself killed the emperor. He seems to be about to confess his crime before Vitellia hushes him:

VITELLIA
>> Tito?

SESTO
>> La nobil alma
>> Versò dal sen trafitto.

SERVILIA, ANNIO, PUBLIO
>> Qual destra rea macchiarsi
>> Potè d'un tal delitto?

SESTO
>> Fu l'uom più scellerato,
>> L'orror della natura,
>> fu ...

VITELLIA
>> Taci, forsennato,
>> Deh non ti palesar! (Mazzolà, Act I, Sc. 14)

VITELLIA
>> Tito?

SESTO
>> His noble soul flowed from his wounded breast.

SERVILIA, ANNIO, PUBLIO
> What wicked hand could have stained itself with such a crime?

SESTO
> It was the wickedest of men, the horror of nature; it was . . .

VITELLIA
> Silence, madman; do not give yourself away!

Thus Mazzolà implicates Sesto much more deeply in the rebellion than Metastasio does; his crime is greater, his shame more painful.

In Metastasio's libretto, Sesto's friend Annio enters only a few moments after Sesto announced to Vitellia Tito's supposed death, with news that Tito is alive and firmly in control of the government. Thus the threat of revolution and assassination, a threat of which most of the characters in the drama were never even aware, has quickly passed.

In Mazzolà's revision both those on stage and in the audience are allowed to believe for quite some time that Tito has been killed by Sesto himself. Mazzolà, in transposing the coup into the finale of his first act, shifted it from a relatively inconspicuous part of the original libretto to a place of prominence, and, more important, he delayed the outcome of the rebellion. The act ends with the soloists and the people of Rome expressing their shock and grief at the news of Tito's death and their outrage at his betrayal:

VITELLIA, SERVILIA, SESTO, ANNIO, PUBLIO
> Ah! dunque l'astro è spento,
> Di pace apportator.

TUTTI e CORO
> Oh nero tradimento,
> Oh giorno di dolor.

VITELLIA, SERVILIA, SESTO, ANNIO, PUBLIO
> Ah, then the star is extinguished, the bringer of peace.

TUTTI and CHORUS
> Oh black betrayal! Oh day of grief!

It is not until after the intermission that the singers and the audience learn that Tito is alive and that the rebellion has failed.

4   *Composition and first performance*

The contract that impresario Domenico Guardasoni signed on 8 July 1791 required that he do much in a very short time. He had to find two first-class *opera seria* singers in Italy and to persuade them to make the long journey to Prague; he had to find a librettist for a new drama or a poet willing to rework Metastasio's *La clemenza di Tito*; and he had to find a "distinguished composer" who was willing to provide the music at top speed and, according to custom, to lead the first few performances. Guardasoni had some singers in Prague. These he could draw on for some of the opera's roles, including that of Tito. But for the *prima donna* and male soprano stipulated by the contract, and for the composer, he went elsewhere. Guardasoni's contract required him to travel to Vienna and to Italy. Vienna was presumably his first stop on his journey south.

Guardasoni first asked Antonio Salieri, Kapellmeister of the imperial court in Vienna, to compose the coronation opera; at least this is what we are led to believe by a recently published letter from Salieri to Prince Anton Esterhazy, Haydn's employer, written probably in August 1791. Salieri described in the letter how busy he was during the summer of 1791, while his student Joseph Weigl was occupied with the composition of a cantata for Prince Esterhazy. (Haydn was in London at the time.) Salieri took over from Weigl many of the tasks connected with the running of the court theaters in Vienna. He was so busy that he had to decline a commission to compose the coronation opera for Prague:

And furthermore, without regretting it however, I declined to write the opera which is being prepared for the coronation in Bohemia, for which opera the impresario of Prague visited me five times to press the commission on me to the point of showing me 200 zecchini, a commission which I could not accept since I alone was attending to the affairs of the Court theater.[1]

45

It was evidently only after Salieri turned him down that Guardasoni offered the commission to Mozart.

Several scholars, some of them quoted in chapter 7, have expressed the view that Mozart accepted the commission for *La clemenza di Tito* reluctantly, that he wrote the opera against his will. This view is closely connected to the widely shared idea that *opera seria* was an old-fashioned genre, even a dying one, in 1791. Many scholars have found it hard to believe that Mozart could actually have wanted to write an *opera seria*.

Mozart devoted himself to the comic stage during his decade in Vienna. Yet this dedication to *opera buffa* should be interpreted not as a dislike for *opera seria* on Mozart's part but as a concession to operatic conditions in Vienna. The absence of *opera seria* from the Burgtheater during the 1780s reflected Joseph II's attitude toward the genre, not Mozart's. Before settling in Vienna in 1781 Mozart spent as much time and effort on serious opera (*Mitridate*, 1770; *Lucio Silla*, 1772; *Idomeneo*, 1781) as on comic. Mozart felt a particular affinity with Italian serious opera. "Do not forget how much I want to write operas," Mozart wrote to his father in 1778. "I envy anyone who is writing one. I could really weep in frustration when I hear or see an aria. But Italian, not German, serious, not *buffa*."[2] There is no reason to believe that Mozart's interest in *opera seria* had lessened by 1791; on the contrary, it is likely that the genre of *La clemenza di Tito* was one of the aspects of the commission that convinced Mozart to accept it.

Another reason why Mozart might have been eager to set *La clemenza di Tito* to music was the favor with which the genre of *opera seria* was being treated by the Viennese court at the time. Leopold's establishment of an *opera seria* troupe in Vienna during 1791 meant that serious opera in Italian would be an important part of the operatic repertory in Vienna during his reign, and that composers who specialized in *opera seria* would be in demand. Mozart would have wanted to be among them.

Mozart sought Leopold's patronage. One of his purposes in travelling to Frankfurt in September 1790 for the festivities celebrating the coronation of Leopold as Holy Roman Emperor was probably to impress upon the emperor his eagerness for court patronage. That was certainly his aim in writing to Leopold's son Archduke Francis (later Emperor Francis II) soon after Leopold's arrival in Vienna, asking the Archduke to intercede with Leopold on his behalf, to secure his promotion to the position of second Kapellmeister.[3]

But Mozart's quest for Leopold's approval and support had begun much earlier. Their lives had touched several times. When, in 1762, the six-year-old Mozart visited Vienna for the first time, he attracted the attention of the fifteen-year-old Archduke Leopold. Leopold Mozart wrote happily from Vienna:

We are in demand everywhere, and when I was in the theater alone on the 10th [of October] I heard Archduke Leopold call out a number of things from his box to another, that a boy was in Vienna who plays the harpsichord so well, and so forth.[4]

Eight years later Mozart and his father passed through Florence, where Archduke Leopold now ruled as Grand Duke of Tuscany. Leopold Mozart wrote to his wife of their grand-ducal audience:

The Grand Duke was uncommonly kind, and asked us immediately about Nannerl. He said that his wife was very eager to hear Wolfgang, and spoke with us for a good quarter of an hour.[5]

Soon thereafter Leopold Mozart applied for a position for his son at Grand Duke Leopold's court. "I have news from Florence," he wrote to his wife, "that the Grand Duke has received my letter, is giving it sympathetic consideration and will let me know the results. We still live in hopes."[6] Late in 1772 Leopold Mozart sent a copy of his son's *Lucio Silla* from Milan: "I have sent Wolfgang's opera to the Grand Duke in Florence. Even if there is no hope of obtaining anything from him, I trust that he will recommend us".[7]

Almost twenty years later Mozart accepted the commission for another *opera seria*. The commission for *Tito* was an opportunity for him to demonstrate once again his willingness to serve Leopold, now emperor; and it was an opportunity for Mozart to demonstrate again his ability to write operas in a genre that Leopold valued in 1791 as highly as he had in 1772.

Problems of chronology

When he accepted the commission (presumably around the middle of July 1791), Mozart probably knew the voice of only one of the singers who would perform his opera: Antonio Baglioni, the first Tito, had created the role of Don Ottavio in *Don Giovanni* four years earlier. Since an eighteenth-century composer was expected to tailor his vocal music to the specifications of the singers who were to perform it, this left Mozart, with less than two months to compose his opera, in a difficult situation. How could he go forward with composition if he knew the voice of only one of his singers?

Mozart's autograph score of *La clemenza di Tito* survives (most of it today is in the Staatsbibliothek Preussischer Kulturbesitz, Berlin), and the paper on which he wrote can tell us much about how he went about composing the opera during the hectic summer of 1791. Alan Tyson has shown that Mozart used five different kinds of paper for the autograph. Studying the distribution of the different kinds of paper throughout the autograph, Tyson points to interesting patterns. For example, Mozart used what Tyson calls Paper-type I for three ensembles as well as for some preliminary sketches for the opera; the rest of the opera is written on other types of paper. Tyson concludes:

The reason why these pieces – early drafts, and completed numbers for two or three voices in the first act – and *only* these (apart from a single leaf with wind parts) are on Paper-type I is surely obvious: they were written before the rest of the opera. If Mozart, badly pressed for time, decided to go ahead with some numbers before he had heard in every case who the singers were to be, it must have struck him as the least risky course to tackle a few of the duets and trios and to leave the solo arias till later.[8]

Following Tyson's argument through four of the five paper-types we arrive at the following sequence.

Without having a clear idea of the cast that was to perform his opera, Mozart began his compositional task, using Paper-type I, with some of the ensembles of Act I: the duet for Sesto and Vitellia "Come ti piace imponi," the duet for Servilia and Annio "Ah perdona il primo affetto," and the trio for Vitellia, Annio, and Publio "Vengo . . . aspettate . . . Sesto!"

Mozart continued to compose, concentrating as before on ensembles, but now using Paper-type II. He wrote the little duettino for Sesto and Annio, "Deh prendi un dolce amplesso," the trio for Sesto, Tito, and Publio "Quello di Tito è il volto?" He wrote the quintet with chorus at the end of Act I and came close to completing the sextet with chorus at the end of Act II. By choosing, at this relatively early point in the compositional process, to write the final ensemble of Act II in C major Mozart assigned to C major the role of the opera's tonal center. He also wrote the two brilliant choruses in praise of Tito, "Serbate, oh dei custodi" for Act I and "Che del ciel, che degli dei" for Act II.

At around the same time, Mozart, still using Paper-type II, began to work on the music for Baglioni. He completed Tito's first aria, "Del più sublime soglio" and the chorus with a solo passage for Tito, "Ah grazie si rendano." He started to compose another aria for Baglioni, "Se all'impero."

Having finally gained some idea of the qualities and limitations of his other singers, Mozart went to work composing their arias and orchestrally-accompanied recitatives, using Paper-type III.

In Prague, shortly before the first performance, Mozart turned to Paper-type V, and composed the march for the entrance of Tito in Act I, a third aria for Tito ("Ah, se fosse intorno al trono"), two segments of accompanied recitative, and, probably last of all, the overture.

According to this scenario Mozart wrote *La clemenza di Tito* in four stages, corresponding to four of the five paper-types that he used in his autograph. But what about Paper-type IV? It appears in only one place in the autograph: Mozart used it to compose the second part, the Allegro section, of his rondò for Vitellia, "Non più di fiori." The opening Larghetto section is written on Paper-type III. Tyson concludes that Mozart wrote the Allegro at some time other than the rest of the opera, and presumably earlier. The Larghetto, on the other hand, was written or revised shortly before the first performance of *Tito*, in August or early September 1791. "Non più di fiori," as it survives today, seems to consist of an aria written earlier than July 1791, which Mozart incorporated into *La clemenza di Tito* around the same time that he wrote the rest of the opera, in the process of which he replaced the opening slow section with a new one.

The problems of "Non più di fiori" and its relation to the rest of *Tito* are important and challenging. The Czech musicologist Tomislav Volek suggested the possibility that Mozart began composing *La clemenza di Tito* long before he received the commission from Guardasoni in July 1791.[9] As evidence he pointed to an announcement of a concert that took place in Prague on 26 April 1791, in which the soprano Josepha Duschek, one of Mozart's closest friends in Prague, sang two of his arias, as well as one by Cimarosa. The concert announcement referred to one of the arias by Mozart as a "rondò with obbligato basset horn." Volek identified this unnamed aria with the only aria with obbligato basset horn that Mozart is known to have composed: "Non più di fiori." He argued further that Mozart wrote "Non più di fiori" not as a concert aria for Josepha Duschek, but with the intention of using it in a setting of Metastasio's libretto *La clemenza di Tito*; in other words, that Mozart began composing the opera much earlier than had previously been believed.

The text of the rondò supports Volek's hypothesis. Its imagery matches well the recitative that precedes it in the opera. Vitellia sings "Non più di fiori" as part of her climactic solo *scena* near the end of the opera. Overcome by desperation and remorse, she decides to confess her guilt to Tito, so giving up her chance to become his wife. Metastasio provided for this scene twenty lines of passionate blank verse and a concluding aria, "Getta il nocchier talora." Mozart set the first fifteen and a half of Metastasio's lines unchanged as an accompanied recitative, which concludes with a line adapted from Metastasio's next words,

> Speranze, addio,
> D'impero e d'imenei!

> Farewell, hopes of empire and marriage!

Mozart's recitative ends:

> D'impero e d'imenei, speranze, addio.

The aria that follows, "Non più di fiori," begins with a quatrain in which the reference to Imene (Hymen, god of marriage) seems to grow out of the word *imenei* in the recitative:

> Non più di fiori
> Vaghe catene
> Discenda Imene
> Ad intrecciar

> Let Hymen no longer descend to weave charming chains of flowers.

The connection between aria-text and recitative suggests that the aria-text was written for this particular context in the opera. If so, then a performance of the aria in April 1791 would mean that Mozart was at that time already at work on *La clemenza di Tito*.[10]

The evidence adduced by Tyson's paper-studies confirms Volek's idea that Mozart wrote "Non più di fiori" (at least some version of it) before July. But it renders less likely Volek's theory that Mozart wrote more than "Non più di fiori" before he received the commission in July 1791. In terms of the paper it is written on, the Allegro section of "Non più di fiori" is clearly isolated from the rest of the opera: there is no indication that any other part of the opera dates from before the summer of 1791. Yet Tyson's analysis still leaves him and his readers wondering how Mozart could have written an aria whose text fits so well into an opera that he had not apparently begun to write.

Mozart's singers

For most of his cast Guardasoni went to members of his own opera troupe, who were specialists in comic opera. In addition to the tenor Antonio Baglioni (Tito) he engaged Carolina Perini (Annio), Gaetano Campi (Publio), and a certain Signora Antonini (Servilia). Perini had sung soprano roles in *opera buffa* in Venice in 1790, including at least one *prima buffa* role (that is, the leading female role in a comic opera). Within a year or two of her performances in *La clemenza di Tito* she returned to Italy and her career as a soprano in comic opera. Of the bass, Campi, we know little except that he was a member of Guardasoni's troupe. Of Signora Antonini, who took the role of Servilia, we know nothing, not even her first name.

Guardasoni was successful in his attempt to coax two of Italy's leading singers to be *prima donna* and *primo musico* in his coronation opera. As *prima donna* he hired Maria Marchetti Fantozzi, a singer of leading female roles in some of Italy's biggest opera houses. As *primo uomo*, Guardasoni hired Domenico Bedini, a male soprano who, if not as famous as Luigi Marchesi or Gasparo Pacchierotti, was nevertheless a distinguished and experienced specialist in serious opera.

Mozart's Vitellia began singing publicly in the early 1780s. Maria Marchetti Fantozzi rose quickly to the first rank of *opera seria* sopranos. By 1790 she was familiar to audiences in many of Italy's leading theaters, including La Scala in Milan and San Carlo in Naples. Marchetti was a specialist in the portrayal of strong, passionate and tragic heroines like Semiramis, Cleopatra, and Dido. She had a big, rich voice and was a skillful actress. A report in the *Gazzetta urbana veneta* praised her acting as well as her singing in the title role of *La morte di Semiramide* (Padua, Fall 1790), with music by Prati and Nasolini: "La Marchetti, who is an excellent actress and a good singer, pleased exceedingly and deservedly."[11]

As a *prima donna* in late eighteenth-century Italy, Marchetti had to be able to execute a type of aria that was normally granted only to the *prima donna* and *primo uomo*, and which audiences often focussed upon as the climactic moment of an opera: the rondò. "Signora Marchetti pleased, and she continues to please infinitely," reported the *Gazzetta urbana veneta* of her performance in Tarchi's *Ademira* in Brescia during the summer of 1790. "Her rondò in the second act is a most beautiful piece executed with consummate mastery and with much spirit."[12]

About two years after creating the role of Vitellia in Mozart's *Tito* Marchetti became *prima donna* at the Royal Opera in Berlin, and excited much praise. The composer Johann Friedrich Reichardt wrote of her performance in Righini's *Enea in Lazio* (Carnival 1793), in which she sang the part of Lavinia:

More astonishing still than Righini's beautiful work ... was Signora Marchetti Fantozzi, whose voice, when I previously heard it in a chamber setting, seemed not to promise what it achieved so beautifully in the theater. It is one of those strong, full voices that dare not let themselves go in the chamber, and therefore sound dull, but which have great effect in a large space, where they can expand and spread out. She filled the entire opera house, and without ever shouting, as Mme. Todi [i.e. the soprano Luisa Todi, previously engaged in Berlin] so often did when she wanted to sing as powerfully as possible. In her appearance too Mme. Marchetti is more heroic and more theatrical, and as actress she seems to surpass Mme. Todi, who herself was such an excellent one. For grand opera I would never be able to imagine a more beautiful combination than the voice, the appearance and the acting of Mme. Marchetti.[13]

Another description in the same journal has more details:

The compass of her voice is not big; the low register is rough and dull and the upper reaches are such that she can reach high C only in passing. Yet her otherwise full voice is completely at her command; her tone is quite pure, and she has the Italian expressivity with its good aspects and without too much exaggeration; she sings with great feeling, and, when it is necessary, with considerable virtuosity, although it requires much effort of her ... But her acting, her delivery are masterful; they are such as only she, the best actress on the operatic stage, can have.[14]

Of Domenico Bedini's voice and musical talents we know less than we do of Marchetti's. Bedini sang many roles during his more than thirty-year career, including settings of most of Metastasio's most famous *drammi per musica*: *Achille in Sciro, Ezio, Demetrio, Demofoonte, Olimpiade, Didone abbandonata, Alessandro nell' Indie*, and *Adriano in Siria* (we have no record, however, of his having sung *La clemenza di Tito* before 1791). Like many eighteenth-century opera singers, Bedini made a specialty of performing certain roles, which he sang in a number of different musical settings. He sang the role of Arsace in at least three productions of Giovanni De Gamerra's libretto *Medonte Re di Epiro*: one anonymous setting (Macerata, 1778), probably a *pasticcio* (an opera with arias by several composers), one setting by Insanguine (Naples, 1779), and one setting by Sarti (Lucca, 1785); and he sang the role of Enea in at least three productions, all of them *pasticci*, of Metastasio's *Didone abbandonata* (Florence, 1786; Genoa, 1787; and Padua, 1791).[15] He almost certainly carried settings of particular arias with him from one of these productions to another.

Bedini's singing and appearance did not please everyone. When William Beckford, admirer and friend of the great *musico* Gasparo Pacchierotti, saw Bedini perform in Florence during the Fall season of 1780, he was disappointed: "Bedini, first soprano, put my patience to severe proof, during the few minutes I attended. You never beheld such a porpoise. If these animals were to sing, I should conjecture it would be in his style."[16] But Bedini must have been a fine soprano, for his long career, which began in the 1760s, took him to most of the operatic centers of Italy. Bedini was popular in Florence, despite Beckford's negative reaction: he sang there in at least six different operas between 1780 and 1786, and his singing was surely familiar to Grand Duke Leopold. Although he was near the end of his career in 1791, Bedini must still have been near the top of his form and, like Marchetti, he must have still been a skillful interpreter of rondòs, to judge from a review of one of his last performances in Italy before he travelled north to Prague. Bedini's singing in Paisiello's *Ipermestra* in Padua during June 1791 was praised by the *Gazzetta urbana veneta*, according to which "he greatly pleased with his rondò."[17]

When Marchetti and Bedini performed together in Prague in September 1791 it was not for the first time. During the Spring of 1785 they shared the stage of the Pergola Theater in Florence, with Marchetti's Aristea opposite Bedini's Megacle in Borghi's *L'Olimpiade* (like Mozart's *Tito* a setting of a revised version of a Metastasio libretto). Marchetti and Bedini sang together again in 1789, appearing during Carnival of that year in Genoa as *prima donna* and *primo uomo* in two *opere serie*. Their experience on the same stage must have come in useful during the hurried rehearsals for *La clemenza di Tito* in Prague.

The singer for whom Mozart wrote the part of Tito, Antonio Baglioni, was a lyric tenor who sang in comic opera in Venice before coming north to Prague in 1787. He was a specialist in the performance of the romantic lead in comic operas, the type of role often referred to in Italy as "primo buffo mezzo carattere." The lyrical music he was expected to sing was in some respects similar to the kind of music sung by tenors in serious opera. And yet in Italy the line between comic opera singers and serious opera singers was very clearly drawn; singers did not often cross it. The great *opera seria* tenors of the day, such as Vincenzo Maffoli and Giovanni Ansani, rarely if ever sang even serious roles in comic operas. And the leading tenors of *opera buffa*, even those who specialized in portraying earnest young lovers, rarely if ever sang in *opera seria*.

North of the Alps this distinction between *opera seria* tenors and *opera buffa* tenors was not so clear.[18] Guardasoni, hastily putting a cast together for *La·clemenza di Tito*, and without anything in his contract requiring him to hire a tenor who specialized in *opera seria*, quite naturally thought of Baglioni for the title role of *La clemenza di Tito*.

Antonio Baglioni as Ottavio and Tito

Since Mozart wrote his arias so carefully to suit the voices of his singers, we should be able to learn much about Mozart's musical craft if we can learn about the limitations and special qualities of the singers for whom he wrote. The music that Mozart wrote for Baglioni to sing in *La clemenza di Tito* is a case in point. We know something of Baglioni's voice and musicianship from the music that Mozart wrote for him in *Don Giovanni*, and in particular from his single aria, "Il mio tesoro." In writing for the same singer four years later, Mozart carefully observed the limits of Baglioni's voice and took advantage of its strengths.

Baglioni's range was not particularly wide. In "Il mio tesoro" he ranged an octave and a fifth, from an isolated D in the bass clef up to an isolated A in the treble clef. His tessitura lay right in the center of this range, the octave centering on middle C. ("Tessitura" is used here to denote that part of the range in which most of the part is written, in which the singer declaims the text, and to which most of the sustained notes and coloratura is limited.) Mozart defined this octave in Baglioni's first phrases (Ex. 1). Within the octave from F to F Baglioni could spin elaborate strands of

Ex. 1

coloratura. With his excellent breath-control, he could hold a note over three measures and then extend the line in a cascade of sixteenth notes (Ex. 2). Several times Mozart gave Baglioni the pitch F above middle C to hold over several measures, an indication that Baglioni could sustain that pitch, at the top of his tessitura, with particular beauty.

Ex. 2

"Il mio tesoro" is in B flat. The fact that Mozart chose B flat for Baglioni's only aria may mean that Baglioni sang particularly effectively in that key. One reason he might have done so is that the sustained Fs Baglioni could apparently sing so well fit nicely into an aria in B flat: as the fifth degree of the B-flat scale, F can be sustained as tonic and dominant harmony alternate below it; this is in fact how the sustained Fs are used in "Il mio tesoro."

It could be argued that characteristics of Baglioni's voice are to be expected in any late eighteenth-century lyric tenor. Yet a glance at the music that Mozart wrote for another tenor who specialized in comic opera, Vincenzo Calvesi, who created the role of Ferrando in *Così fan tutte*, suggests that Calvesi's voice was quite different from Baglioni's.[19] Calvesi's range and tessitura were about as wide as Baglioni's, but somewhat higher; his tone at the top of the tessitura was brilliant; but he does not seem to have had either Baglioni's extraordinary breath-control or his capacity for coloratura.

Calvesi might have found "Il mio tesoro" difficult, if not impossible to sing, just as Baglioni had trouble with the role of Ferrando. A report dated December 1794 concerning opera in Prague, by Franz Xaver Niemetschek (who was later to write the first substantial biography of Mozart), harshly criticized Baglioni and claimed that he could not sing the role of Ferrando. Niemetschek called him a "mezzo basso," in reference, no doubt, to his comparatively low tessitura:

This artist left the company a year ago and spent some time in Italy; here he diligently acquired all the bad habits of Italian artists and non-artists, and thus favoured he returned to Signor Guardasoni. He sings not one note as the composer wrote it and expected it, he drowns the most beautiful thoughts with his Italian runs and trills and allows his uniform method of gesticulating with his hands to serve for action, so that one is hard pressed to recognize the aria he is singing. Of course he is in need of such fripperies to disguise his defective voice, which is more of a mezzo basso; but because Signor Baglioni cannot cope with his arias in Mozart's *Così fan tutte*, he should not give out that for this reason the arias are badly written: for the great Mozart, whose spirit is too incomprehensible for flighty Italians, did not take Signor Baglioni as his standard when composing.[20]

But Mozart did indeed take Signor Baglioni as his standard when composing music for the title role in *La clemenza di Tito*. Mozart wrote three arias for Baglioni. The last, "Se all'impero," is the longest, most difficult, and dramatically most important: in it Tito celebrates the triumph of his clemency over his feelings of disappointment and anger. Mozart chose the key of B flat for "Se all'impero," thus saving the key of "Il mio tesoro" for Baglioni's most difficult aria. Mozart likewise saved for this aria the coloratura that he knew Baglioni was capable of, but which is completely absent from the two other arias. The sustained F that Baglioni could apparently sing so beautifully makes an appearance here too: F is the only pitch that Mozart asked Baglioni to sustain for a whole measure in "Se all'impero."

Mozart defined the limits of Baglioni's tessitura, the octave from F below middle C to F above, in the opening melody of "Il mio tesoro," and then expanded the range up a little further, to G, in subsequent phrases. Mozart did exactly the same in the opening measures of "Se all'impero" (Ex. 3). The highest note in "Il mio tesoro" is an isolated A later in the aria; in "Se all'impero" Mozart asked Baglioni to go a little higher: he gave him two isolated B flats to sing near the end.

Writing for the singer for whom he had written "Il mio tesoro," Mozart returned not only to the key, the coloratura, and the range

Ex. 3

Ex. 4

Ex. 5

of the earlier aria, but also to some of its melodic, harmonic, and accompanimental ideas. He began one of the most elaborate of Baglioni's coloratura passages (Ex. 4) in the same harmonic context as one of the coloratura passages in "Il mio tesoro" (Ex. 5).

The coloratura of the two passages is also related, as is the accompaniment, in which winds and strings alternate in dialogue.

The violins play the opening part of "Il mio tesoro" with mutes, contributing to its tender, gentle effect. The removal of mutes coincides with the aria's first *forte* and a sudden plunge to G minor. Dotted rhythms in the vocal line express Ottavio's strength of mind as he promises to avenge the wrongs committed against Donna Anna (Ex. 6). Equally dramatic is the moment at the end of "Se all'impero" where an equally unexpected detour, again to G minor, serves as a transition to the march-like coda (Ex. 7). The vocal line, descending from G in dotted rhythms, and the harmonic destination of F major (although reached by means different from those in the earlier aria) both echo "Il mio tesoro."

"Se all'impero" was the result of collaborations: not only of Mozart and Metastasio (who wrote the text) but also of Mozart and

Ex. 6

Ex. 7

Baglioni. The singer's influence affected many of the composer's decisions; much of the special character of "Se all'impero" comes from the character of the singer for whom it was written.

Anton Stadler and his clarinets

Another musician for whom Mozart wrote music in *La clemenza di Tito* and whose skills helped to shape the opera was the clarinettist Anton Stadler, a member of Vienna's Burgtheater orchestra. Stadler was one of Mozart's closest friends – a fellow Mason and a musician whom Mozart seems to have greatly respected. It was for Stadler that Mozart wrote most of his greatest works for clarinet, including the Quintet K. 581 and the Concerto K. 622.[21]

Stadler apparently shared with Mozart a special interest in the clarinet's lowest register. In addition to his regular clarinets he played the basset horn, a tenor clarinet of which Mozart too was fond, and which may have had Masonic associations. Mozart used basset horns in the Masonic Funeral Music, the Requiem, *Die Zauberflöte*, the great Adagio for two clarinets and three basset horns K. 411, and several other works. Stadler also experimented with instruments whose range extended a major third below those of the regular clarinets in A and B flat, the so-called "basset-clarinets." Mozart's clarinet parts in the Quintet and the Concerto indicate that he wrote them for Stadler to play on a basset-clarinet.

Mozart and Stadler were particularly close in 1791. The Clarinet Concerto, completed by Mozart around the beginning of October 1791, was his last orchestral composition. He may have intended one of the Requiem's basset horn parts for Stadler. Earlier in the year Mozart wrote for Stadler elaborate basset-clarinet and basset horn parts in two of the most important arias in *La clemenza di Tito*, "Parto, ma tu, ben mio" (for basset-clarinet) and "Non più di fiori" (for basset horn).

Both arias make brilliant use of Stadler's artistry. The slow, lyrical clarinet melodies, the chromatic passages, the wide variety of arpeggiated patterns, the deep, rich sonorities produced by both basset-clarinet and basset horn: all these features of "Parto, ma tu, ben mio" and "Non più di fiori" are familiar to all those who know the Clarinet Quintet and the Clarinet Concerto. Their presence in two of *La clemenza di Tito*'s greatest arias is the result not only of Mozart's own interest in the clarinet, but also of his response to Stadler's talents.

The performance in Prague

H. C. Robbins Landon has described in vivid detail the events in Prague leading to the coronation of Leopold as King of Bohemia and to the performance of Mozart's *La clemenza di Tito* on the evening of coronation day.[22] Mozart and his wife arrived in Prague on 28 August, accompanied by Franz Xaver Süssmayr, the student and assistant who probably came to Prague to help Mozart with copying, proofreading, and rehearsals. The next few days must have been full of last-minute composing for Mozart, and probably for Süssmayr as well; for it is likely that Süssmayr composed most of the simple recitative. With the exception of a few measures, Mozart's autograph score of *La clemenza di Tito* contains no simple recitative. A report of the opera's premiere in the *Musikalisches Wochenblatt* of Berlin, published shortly after the event, claimed that "only the arias and choruses were by his [Mozart's] hand; the recitatives were by another."[23] If this report is true, it is likely that Süssmayr was the unnamed composer of the simple recitative, since he was in Prague when the opera was being prepared.

Meanwhile the court and aristocracy made an endless round of receptions, processions and ceremonies, and passed the evenings in banquets, plays, concerts, and operas. Guardasoni's troupe, although some of its members may have already been busy with rehearsals for *Tito*, had time to present Paisiello's serious opera *Pirro* on 29 August, the day after Mozart's arrival; on 2 September the troupe performed Mozart's *Don Giovanni* in the presence of the imperial family. This series of events came to a climax on

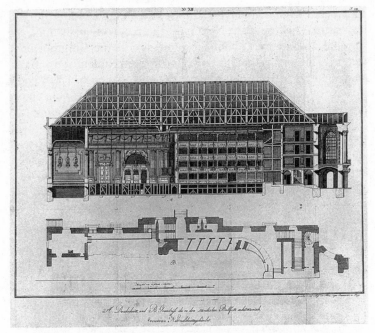

4   The National Theater in Prague, as decorated for the Coronation
Ball organized by the Bohemian Estates, 12 September 1791.
Longitudinal cross-section and ground plan by Filip and Franz Heger

6 September, with the coronation of Leopold and the performance
of the coronation opera.

Mozart's compositional task seems to have continued up to the
previous day; he entered the opera in his manuscript thematic
catalogue under the date 5 September:

the 5th September. – performed in *Prague on 6th September*. La clemenza
di Tito. Opera seria in two acts for the coronation of His Majesty Emperor
Leopold II. – reduced to true opera by Sig[no]re Mazzolà, poet of His
Serene Highness the Elector of Saxony. *Actresses: Sig[no]ra Marchetti
Fantozi. Sig[no]ra Antonini. – Actors: Sig[no]re Bedini. Sig[no]ra Carolina Perini* (as a man). *Sig[no]re Baglioni. Sig[no]re Campi.* – and
choruses. – 24 numbers.[24]

The opera was performed in a theater that still stands in the
center of Prague and is known today as the Tyl Theater (Plate 4).[25]
The Bohemian nobleman Count Franz Anton Nostitz Rieneck,
Supreme Burgrave and Governor-General of Bohemia, had the
theater built in 1782 to an elegant neo-classical design by Anton

Hafenecker. The theater was known in the eighteenth century as the Nostitz-Theater or the Nationaltheater. As originally built, the National Theater was about the same size as the Burgtheater in Vienna. This means that it was rather small in comparison with the great theaters of Italy. La Scala in Milan (opened in 1778) had a capacity of about 3000; the National Theater in Prague held "more than a thousand persons," according to one contemporary account.[26] The auditorium was about eighteen meters long, with room for about twenty benches or rows of seats, and about twelve meters wide. The sides, parallel to one another, with three tiers of boxes, extended back to a rounded end. The stage was a big one, extending back almost as far as the length of the auditorium. The proscenium was almost square: about eleven meters both in width and in height.[27]

Jiří Hilmera describes the National Theater's decoration:

... the parapets of the boxes were covered by panels with classicist festoons, above each box were garlands of flowers, the ceiling of the gallery was supported by caryatids; in the middle of the dress circle was the box of honour under a baldachin crowned by plumes; decorative draperies spread to the two adjoining boxes to form an architectural whole with the box of honour. The proscenium was flanked by white neoclassicist pilasters with gilded details and topped by a coffered lintel supported by huge volutes. Above the proscenium arch was a medallion with a portrait of Gotthold Effraim Lessing in relief. This corresponded to the choice of Lessing's *Emilia Galotti* for the opening performance at the new theatre and symbolized the intentions of the management – high literary quality and progressive ideas.[28]

It was in this beautiful National Theater that the music-lovers of Prague enthusiastically applauded *Le nozze di Figaro* in 1786; here that *Don Giovanni* was performed for the first time the following year. And it was here, on 6 September 1791, in the brilliant light of innumerable candles, before an audience dressed in a festive array of bright colors, rich cloth, and sparkling jewelry, that Mozart presented *La clemenza di Tito* to Leopold, newly crowned King of Bohemia (Plate 5).

Count Johann Karl Zinzendorf, a high government official from Vienna and an enthusiastic theater-goer, left us a description of the first performance of *La clemenza di Tito* in his diary:

At 5 o'clock to the theater in the Old Town, to the spectacle that the Estates are presenting. I was put in a box in the first tier. [There follows mention of some of the dignitaries who shared Zinzendorf's box, and of some of the acquaintances he saw in other boxes.] The court did not arrive

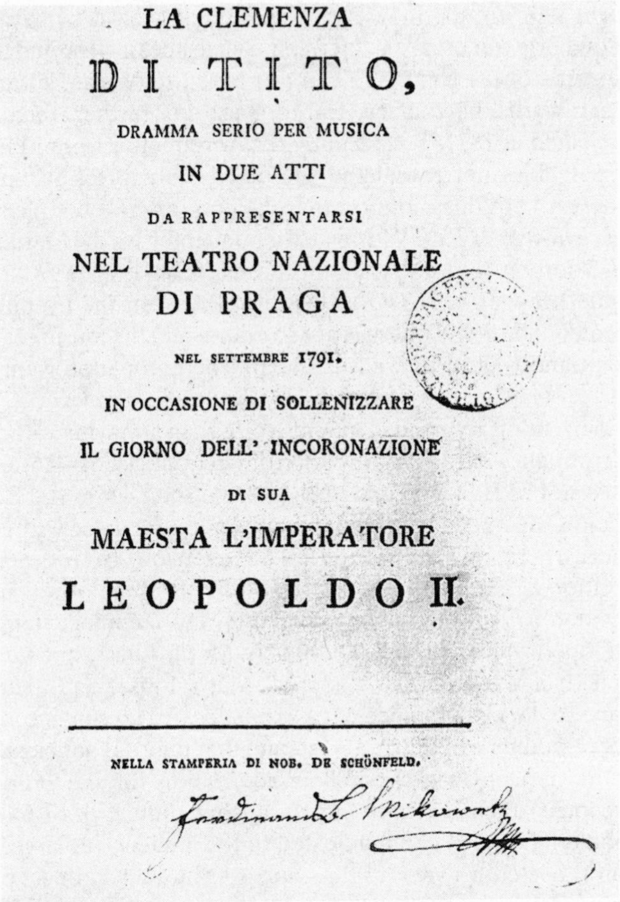

LA CLEMENZA

DI TITO,

DRAMMA SERIO PER MUSICA

IN DUE ATTI

DA RAPPRESENTARSI

NEL TEATRO NAZIONALE
DI PRAGA

NEL SETTEMBRE 1791.

IN OCCASIONE DI SOLLENIZZARE

IL GIORNO DELL' INCORONAZIONE

DI SUA

MAESTA L'IMPERATORE

LEOPOLDO II.

NELLA STAMPERIA DI NOB. DE SCHÖNFELD.

5   Title page of the libretto for the first production: "'La clemenza di Tito,' serious drama for music in two acts, to be performed in the National Theater of Prague in September 1791, on the occasion of the celebration of the coronation of His Majesty the Emperor Leopold II."

until half past seven. We were presented with the most boring spectacle, *La clemenza di Tito*. Rotenhan was in the box with the Emperor ... Marchetti sings very well; the Emperor is enthusiastic about her. It was extremely difficult getting out of this theater ...[29]

Zinzendorf was not the only member of the audience disappointed by *La clemenza di Tito*. Empress Maria Luisa, whose birthday would be celebrated later that year with the debut of Leopold's *opera seria* troupe in Vienna, also found Mozart's opera boring. "Porcheria tedesca" – German swinishness: this judgment of Mozart's opera has long been attributed to Maria Luisa, but the exact words have been traced back no further than a book published in 1871.[30] A recently recovered letter from Maria Luisa herself does not reveal the source of the expression "porcheria tedesca," but does confirm that the empress was not pleased with *La clemenza di Tito*. Writing to her daughter-in-law Maria Theresa de Bourbon the day after the premiere in Prague, Maria Luisa made her views on *Tito* absolutely clear: "In the evening to the theater. The grand opera is not so grand, and the music very bad, so that almost all of us went to sleep. The coronation went marvelously.'[31]

Zinzendorf referred to Count Rottenhan as having witnessed the performance of Mozart's opera from Leopold's box. Rottenhan, as governor of Bohemia and presider over the Diet of the Bohemian Estates, had helped to organize the opera. He later wrote that "at court there was a preconceived aversion to Mozart's composition."[32] Sitting in the imperial box, Rottenhan was in a good position to perceive such an aversion. His comment suggests that the opera failed to please not only Maria Luisa, but Leopold as well. If it was true that Leopold, Maria Luisa, and their retinue came to the performance of *La clemenza di Tito* convinced that the opera would be of little interest, and that they did not like the opera or its performance (Leopold's admiration for the *prima donna* excepted) then it is not surprising that their lack of enthusiasm should have been communicated to the audience at large. Rottenhan reported his view of the court's attitude in connection with a petition for financial support from Guardasoni, who had complained that low attendance at performances of *La clemenza di Tito* after the opening night had caused him to lose money. Rottenhan's implication was that the court's hostility to the opera caused it to fail with the public of Prague.

Another discussion of the first performance of *La clemenza di Tito*, by Niemetschek, provides further insight into the reception of the opera:

It was given at the time of the coronation as a gratis opera, and several more times thereafter; but as fate willed it, a pitiful castrato and a *prima donna* who sang more with her hands than in her throat, and whom one had to consider a lunatic, sang the principal parts; since the subject is too simple to be able to interest the mass of people occupied with coronation festivities, balls and illuminations; and since finally it is – shame on our age – a serious opera, it pleased less, in general, than its truly heavenly music deserved.[33]

Niemetschek's criticism of the *prima donna* and the *primo uomo* does not fit in well with other accounts. Zinzendorf mentioned that Leopold was delighted with Marchetti; and Mozart himself said that both Marchetti and Bedini were warmly applauded when they sang the opera for the last time at the end of September. But it may be true that the coronation festivities distracted audiences from the beauty of Mozart's score.

A discussion of *La clemenza di Tito* in the *Krönungsjournal für Prag*, published shortly after the coronation, praised the opera but not whole-heartedly: with its references to the haste with which the opera was written and the illness that hampered Mozart's work, it seems defensive: "The composition is by the famous Mozart, and does him honour, though he did not have much time for it and was also the victim of an illness, during which he had to complete the last part of the same."[34]

But if the first performance of *La clemenza di Tito* was unsuccessful, audiences in Prague began to appreciate it quickly. Performances continued through the month of September, and the opera seems to have won more and more applause. Mozart wrote to his wife in early October that the final performance of *Tito* was a great success. He reported to her news he had received from the clarinettist Stadler:

And the strangest thing of all is that on the very evening when my new opera [*Die Zauberflöte*] was performed for the first time with such success [30 September 1791], "Tito" was given in Prague for the last time with tremendous applause. Bedini sang better than ever. The little duet in A major ["Ah perdona al primo affetto"] which the two girls [Carolina Perini as Annio and Signora Antonini as Servilia] sing was repeated; and had not the audience wished to spare Marchetti, a repetition of the rondò ["Non più di fiori"] would have been very welcome. Cries of "Bravo" were shouted at Stodla [Stadler] from the parterre and even from the orchestra – "What a miracle for Bohemia," he writes, "but indeed I *did my very best*."[35]

5   *Synopsis and commentary*

The opera that Mozart presented to Emperor Leopold II and the audience of dignitaries assembled in Prague to celebrate his coronation on 6 September 1791 is set in imperial Rome in the year A.D. 79. Vitellia (soprano; the role was created by Maria Marchetti Fantozzi), a patrician woman whose seductive beauty and charm is excelled only by her ambition and ruthlessness, is daughter of the former emperor Vitellius, deposed ten years earlier by Vespasian. Vespasian's son Titus (Tito in the opera; tenor; the role was created by Antonio Baglioni) is now emperor, and Vitellia's hopes of becoming empress as Tito's wife have been disappointed by Tito's love affair with Berenice, princess of Judea. The patrician Sesto (soprano; the role was created by the *musico* Domenico Bedini), a friend of Tito, loves Vitellia; and she, by exploiting his passion, has convinced him, despite his friendship with Tito and his admiration for the emperor's virtue, to lead a rebellion and to assassinate Tito.

The overture

The overture (C major) foreshadows the drama to come, as Daniel Heartz has demonstrated.[1] This is a coronation opera, a glorification of the monarch and his power. At the same time it deals with darker themes: betrayal, vengeance, violence. The overture brings together these opposing aspects of the drama. It opens with a brilliant fanfare, orchestrated with trumpets and drums (Ex. 8). Confident, solid, and majestic, this opening evokes the power and stability of absolute monarchy. Yet the development section, in its harmonic instability, its hectic progress and its harsh dissonances, seems to allude to the pain and confusion, the uncertainty and struggle that lie at the heart of the opera.

The overture also establishes the opera's principal tonal areas.

Ex. 8

C major is the opera's tonal center, the key around which the opera is organized and to which, in the end, it will return. The expotion's second-theme area is of course in G major, the dominant of C. G major will likewise play an important role throughout the opera, as the key of no less than five numbers: three arias, a trio, and a chorus. By emphasizing the key of E flat major at the beginning of the development section, the overture anticipates the emergence, later in the opera, of E flat as a crucial tonal area: the key of the massive first-act finale.

The opening fanfare leads to the overture's most important thematic idea (Ex. 9). This idea consists of two overlapping phrases, labelled x and y in the musical example; the staccato phrase x, played *piano*, is full of nervous energy; it is answered by syncopated y, played *forte*, impetuous and unstable in character. This pair of phrases provides the material out of which Mozart builds his violent development section. And these phrases will be

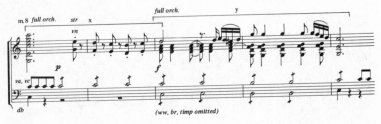

Ex. 9

important later in the opera too, returning, transformed, in some of its most dramatic moments.

A modulatory passage with descending scales in thirds and sixths moves to the dominant much more abruptly than is normal in Mozart's sonata-form movements: the modulatory passage is only fourteen measures long. Perhaps this brevity is a product of the haste with which Mozart was forced to write the overture. (Also possibly symptomatic of haste is the extent to which the thematic material of this overture is indebted to Mozart's earlier music, much of it written in 1780 and 1781. The opening measure is almost identical to the beginning of his Symphony in C, K. 338, composed in Salzburg in 1780 (Ex. 10). The continuation, with its ascent through the tonic triad in martial dotted rhythms, is closely related to the opening measures of the overture to *Idomeneo* (1781); and the second theme (Ex. 11), as Erik Smith has pointed out, harkens back to Mozart's setting of the words "Et exultavit spiritus meus dominum" in the Magnificat that concludes the *Vesperae solennes de confessore* (1780; Ex. 12).)[2]

The development section is announced by a sudden modulation from G major to E flat, the first of several sudden modulations up and down a third that will accompany outbursts of emotion later in the opera. The development takes up phrase x and weaves it into an elaborate polyphonic fabric. From the opening E flat chord a

Ex. 10

Ex. 11

Ex. 12

beautifully fashioned contrapuntal passage leads, with a steadily increasing sense of urgency, to the climax of the overture: a tumultuous eruption of the full orchestra, *forte*, with one intense dissonance after another. Phrases x and y reappear, but now they take on a menacing quality. By transposing the syncopations of phrase y to the highest register and intensifying the harmony with diminished seventh chords Mozart transforms the syncopations into anguished cries.

In the recapitulation we find Mozart using a formal procedure that is rare in his works: this is a reverse recapitulation, with the second theme presented before the first. Perhaps this is another product of Mozart's haste: the reverse recapitulation allowed him to keep connecting material to a minimum. It gives the overture a symmetry that anticipates symmetrical aspects of the opera as a whole. A restatement of the overture's opening material leads to a festive conclusion. The descending scales first presented in the exposition's modulatory passage are now combined with ascending scales; the effect is much like peals of coronation bells.

Act I

Scenes 1–3: Vitellia's residence

The curtain rises to reveal Sesto and Vitellia alone (Plate 6). In his opening dialogue Metastasio acquaints the audience with the background to the story and skillfully sketches the characters of his *primo uomo* and *prima donna*: the former torn between his love for a beautiful woman and his love for sovereign and friend, the latter obsessively focussed on a single goal, to be attained at any price, untroubled by the normal ambiguities of human feelings and

6   Carol Vaness as Vitellia and Tatiana Troyanos as Sesto in
Jean-Pierre Ponnelle's production at the Metropolitan Opera, 1987

human aspirations. Sesto now has second thoughts, praising Tito in
words that echo Suetonius:

> Ah, non togliamo in Tito
> La sua delizia al mondo, il padre a Roma,
> L'amico a noi. Fra le memorie antiche
> Trova l'egual, se puoi. Fingiti in mente
> Eroe più generoso, e più clemente.

> Ah, let us not take from the world its delight, from Rome its father, from ourselves our friend. Find his equal in the memories of antiquity, if you can. Try to imagine a more generous, a more clement hero.

Sesto's eloquent praise of Tito only increases Vitellia's rage and thirst for vengeance; Sesto finally submits.

This dialogue, like most of the dialogue in *La clemenza di Tito*, is sung in simple recitative. The composer of most of this recitative is likely to have been Süssmayr, and it has come in for some harsh criticism.[3] But if Mozart had set the recitative himself it would probably have been quite similar to the setting that we have, for the conventionality of the musical language of simple recitative did not leave composers with much room for originality. This conventionality has been clearly demonstrated by the German musicologist Helga Lühning, who compared the settings of Metastasio's opening lines made by several composers over a period of forty years. The similarities between Gluck's setting (Naples 1752) and the setting in Mozart's opera are not in any way exceptional (Ex. 13).[4] The composer of the recitative in Mozart's opera did not have to know Gluck's setting to arrive at such similar music. Opera composers spoke a common musical language of recitative: they all reacted in similar ways to the phrase structure, line-length, and pace of Metastasio's blank verse. The listener's attention, undistracted by

Ex. 13

musical innovation, is completely dominated by Metastasio's poetry, and by the passion and conviction with which the singer-actor delivers it.

Mazzolà fashioned the duet "Come ti piace imponi" out of the last few lines of Metastasio's dialogue, as we saw in chapter 3. Mozart, in his setting (F major), developed Metastasio's characterizations. Sesto begins the duet, singing a noble line, tender, dignified (Ex. 14). Vitellia's music is impetuous. The accompaniment is agitated, the tonality unstable (Ex. 15). Sesto responds, and the violins' scurrying triplets at m. 25 reflect his growing enthusiasm (Ex. 16). In the concluding Allegro both Sesto and Vitellia express their excitement with rests between syllables, as sudden leaps and syncopations give the music a breathless quality (Ex. 17).

Annio (soprano; in Prague the role was sung by Carolina Perini), another patrician and a friend of Sesto, enters to announce that Tito, obedient to his subjects' unwillingness to have a foreign

Ex. 14

Ex. 15

Ex. 16

Ex. 17

princess on the throne, has broken off his relations with Berenice; she has left Rome. Vitellia sees opportunity for herself in this news; she tells Sesto to postpone the rebellion. Sesto protests at being manipulated thus by Vitellia, and she, in her exit-aria "Deh se piacer mi vuoi" (text by Metastasio, G major) reveals more of her character. In the opening Larghetto she is an ingenuous charmer, coaxing, seductive (Ex. 18). In the concluding Allegro Vitellia delivers with light-hearted glee a stern Metastasian maxim (Ex. 19).

Annio loves Servilia (soprano; the role was sung in Prague by the otherwise unknown Signora Antonini), Sesto's sister, and wants to marry her. As soon as Vitellia has left the stage Annio asks Sesto to help him gain the emperor's approval of his wedding plans. Sesto happily agrees to help; he would be delighted if his friendship with Annio were to be strengthened by the ties of marriage. Sesto and Annio sing a short duet, "Deh prendi un dolce amplesso," another addition by Mazzolà, that expresses their feelings of friendship. The sweet, folklike quality of Mozart's setting (C major) contrasts

Ex. 18

Ex. 19

Ex. 20

vividly with the elaborate, rhetorical duet of Sesto and Vitellia; the rocking 6/8 meter gives this music a gentle, pastoral quality (Ex. 20).

With this duet Mozart completes a large-scale tonal progression, having moved from C major (the overture), to F ("Come ti piace imponi"), to G ("Deh se piacer mi vuoi"), and back to C. This tonic-subdominant-dominant-tonic progression contributes to the solid, monumental quality of *Tito*. Not only does it consolidate C major as the opera's tonal center, it also represents one half of a symmetrical structure that helps to unify the whole opera: the same progression is played out again on an even grander scale in the opera's final scenes.

Scenes 4–5: the Forum

A change of scene reveals, in the words of the libretto, "part of the Roman Forum, splendidly adorned with arches, obelisks and trophies; opposite, the exterior of the Capitol, and the magnificent roadway that leads up to it." The sounds of a triumphal march in E-flat major, with trumpets and drums heard for the first time since the overture, follow directly after the duettino in C; this is the first time in the opera that one orchestrally-accompanied number follows another without intervening recitative. By juxtaposing C major and E flat major Mozart emphasizes on a small scale a tonal relationship that is present in the opera on a much larger scale: as the key of the first-act finale, E flat serves as a foil to the opera's tonal center.

The march accompanies a procession of dignitaries: first Publio (bass; the role was created by Gaetano Campi), the praetorian prefect and Tito's advisor and confidant, then senators, then ambassadors of peoples subjugated by the Romans. Tito himself enters, together with Annio and Sesto, and followed by crowds of people, who sing a brilliant chorus in praise of the emperor, "Serbate, oh dei custodi" (text by Metastasio, but abbreviated, E-flat major).

Dotted rhythms in the vocal and accompanimental parts convey festive, military associations here, as in many other parts of the opera (the overture's opening fanfare, for example). But it may be possible to distinguish a more specific, meaningful rhythmic-melodic motive in this chorus. The opening gesture, a melodic ascent from the first degree to the third in martial dotted rhythms (Ex. 21), reappears elsewhere in the opera, most noticeably in two of Tito's three arias. It gradually takes on a particular meaning, an association with Tito's *impero* (empire, authority, power) and with Tito's ambivalent feelings towards his *impero*.

Ex. 21

Publio announces the Senate's intention of erecting a temple for the worship of the deified Tito. The emperor responds, and in his first words he states his magnanimous credo:

> Romani, unico oggetto
> È de' voti di Tito il vostro amore.

> Romans, the only object of Tito's desires is your love.

He asks that the riches collected for the construction of the temple be put to better use. Vesuvius has just erupted, spreading destruction and death. Let the money be used to help the victims of that disaster; that, says Tito, is the way to build a temple in his honor. He orders the crowds to disperse, and Sesto and Annio to remain. A repetition of the march accompanies the departing crowds.

Before Sesto has a chance to ask Tito for approval for the wedding of Annio and Servilia, the emperor announces to Sesto and Annio his intention of marrying Servilia himself. Sesto and Annio are stunned. Annio hides his feelings; he does not want to keep Servilia from obtaining the position of empress, even if it means that he will lose her. He tells Tito that he has made an excellent choice, and leaves, broken-hearted, to tell Servilia that Tito has chosen her for his bride.

Tito, alone with Sesto, promises that Sesto will, as his future brother-in-law, enjoy all the privileges and benefits of sovereignty. When Sesto protests that too much generosity will make his subjects unappreciative, Tito asks in response:

> Ma che? se mi niegate
> Che benefico io sia, che mi lasciate?

> But what of it? If you deprive me of my generosity, what then have I left?

In his first aria, "Del più sublime soglio" (text by Metastasio), Tito praises generosity as the single satisfaction of his position; everything else is torment and servitude. This aria has reminded several scholars of *Die Zauberflöte*. There is something of Sarastro's nobility in Tito's music. Hermann Abert and several more recent

Ex. 22

(Larghetto)

In dies - en heil' - gen Hal - len

Ex. 23

Ex. 24

Ex. 25

scholars have pointed to melodic connections between Tito's opening line (Ex. 22) and that of Sarastro's "In diesen heil'gen Hallen" (Ex. 23). Abert pointed to another feature that these arias share: the dialogue between the violins and bass-line at the words "tormento e servitù" (Ex. 24) finds a parallel in Sarastro's aria (Ex. 25).[5] Daniel Heartz cited this parallel in support of his argument that Mozart conceived Tito as well as Sarastro as a personification of Masonic benevolence:

Both passages start from a unison and gradually increase the number of voice parts in the texture, an opening outwards that is like a beautiful flower coming into bloom ... The exquisite contrapuntal writing in each instance is emblematic ... Counterpoint bestows solemnity and wisdom on these worthy men.[6]

The nobility and serene beauty of this aria is enhanced by the irony of the situation: Tito sings in praise of princely benevolence to a man who is about to lead an attempt to assassinate him.

After Tito and Sesto have left the stage, Annio enters, and then Servilia. Annio addresses her not as his sweetheart but as his empress, and struggles to tell her his dreadful news. He forgets himself and calls her "anima mia," and, in the love-duet "Ah perdona al primo affetto" (text by Mazzolà, A major) Annio begins by apologizing for his lapse in decorum. His melody, richly harmonized, has a nostalgic sweetness (Ex. 26). But Servilia is not about to abandon Annio for the imperial throne. She repeats Annio's melody but with different words, words that are moving in their simplicity and sincerity:

> Ah tu fosti il primo oggetto,
> Che finor fedel amai,
> E tu l'ultimo sarai,
> Ch'abbia nido in questo cor.
>
> You were the first one I have loved, always faithfully, and you will be the last to have a nesting-place in my heart.

In the fourth and final stanza (borrowed by Mazzolà from one of his comic operas, as was noted in chapter 3), Servilia and Annio join together in tender praise of love.

The orchestration of this duet calls for attention. This is the only number in the opera with parts for woodwinds (flute, pairs of oboes, and bassoons), but no horns. In his other operas Mozart occasionally omitted horns from his orchestral wind ensembles, sometimes in order to call attention to some novel orchestral effect (for example, the piccolo and flute playing in unison – not octaves – in the aria for Monostatos "Alles fühlt der Liebe Freuden," in *Die Zauberflöte*), and sometimes, in ensembles for treble voices, to give the music an especially light quality of sound (the trio for the three boys in *Die Zauberflöte* "Seid uns zum zweiten Mal willkommen," the duettino for the countess and Susanna "Sull'aria" in *Le nozze di Figaro*). In "Ah perdona al primo affetto" the absence of horns helps listeners hear Mozart's interesting use of bassoon and flute. Annio and Servilia, both sopranos, sing the opening melody in turn, both in the same key and register. Both are accompanied by the strings, with the first violins playing the melody in unison with the voice. But Mozart does not allow us to forget that the characters singing this duet are a man and woman; he distinguishes their

Ex. 26

gender subtly and effectively by having a single bassoon accompany Annio, playing his melody an octave below, and having the flute accompany Servilia, playing her melody an octave above.

Scenes 6–10: a secluded garden

Tito and Publio discuss public policy. Publio presents the emperor with a list of those who have slandered the memory of former emperors. Tito orders that the barbarous practice of compiling such lists be abolished. When Publio points out that one offender dared slander the name of Tito himself, the emperor responds with expansive generosity:

> E che perciò? se'l mosse
> Legerezza, nol curo;
> Se follia, lo compiango;
> Se ragion, gli son grato; e se in lui sono
> Impeti di malizia, io gli perdono.[7]

> And what of it? If thoughtlessness caused him to do it, I do not care. If madness, I pity him. If he had good reason, I am grateful to him. And if he was driven by malice, then I forgive him.

The emperor and his minister are interrupted by Servilia. She tells Tito that she is honored by his matrimonial intentions, but that she loves Annio; if Tito insists on marrying her, she will comply, but it is better that he know her true feelings before he makes a final decision.

Tito is delighted both by Servilia's honesty and by the generosity that Annio demonstrated in keeping secret his love for Servilia. He will bless their wedding, and in return, he asks only that Servilia inspire others with her sincerity. In his exuberant aria "Ah se fosse intorno al trono" (text by Metastasio, D major) Tito rejoices in Servilia's honesty, referring, as in his first aria, to the duties of rule as "torment" as long as the ruler is surrounded by deceit.

A remarkable feature of this aria is Mozart's introduction of a new, march-like idea near the end, at the words "un vasto impero," accompanied by horns and oboes in dotted rhythms (Ex. 27). But is this idea in fact new? It is the "*impero* motive" already heard in the chorus "Serbate, oh dei custodi" (see Ex. 21 above). Its re-appearance here is apt. As Tito thinks of the happiness with which he would exercise his authority if his subjects were all as honest as Servilia, the music recalls the joy with which his subjects sang his praises in the chorus.

After Tito leaves, Vitellia enters. Believing that Servilia has agreed to marry Tito, Vitellia spitefully asks for permission to pay her respects to the empress-to-be. Servilia, as she departs, responds that Vitellia herself may become the sovereign's wife. Vitellia imputes to others her own maliciousness; she takes Servilia's encouraging remark as an insult.

Vitellia directs her anger toward Sesto, who happens to enter at that moment. Forgetting that she has recently asked him to postpone the rebellion, Vitellia scolds Sesto violently. She goads him with revolutionary rhetoric ("Io ti propongo la patria a liberar"), taunts him with the suggestion that Tito is his rival in love, and finally demands in disgust that he leave her sight. Sesto, completely overwhelmed by this passionate harangue, promises to do whatever Vitellia demands. But, on the point of leaving to start the rebellion, he once again delays.

Vitellia asks Sesto why he does not leave; he answers with the aria "Parto, ma tu, ben mio" (text by Metastasio with alterations by Mazzolà, B flat major), in which he asks Vitellia to make peace with him before he goes; with but a glance from her he will gladly go to avenge her. Sesto sings Adagio, the same tempo with which he begins his other aria, "Deh per questo istante solo." He is the only character in *La clemenza di Tito* to whom Mozart gave music this slow; Domenico Bedini must have been able to sing long, slow lines with special beauty and pathos. His voice intertwined with the lovely clarinet solo that Mozart wrote for his friend Anton Stadler, Sesto projects a feeling of tender melancholy.

Ex. 27

Ex. 28

A change in tempo to Allegro coincides with Sesto's increasing insistence that Vitellia look at him. The close connection between Mozart's setting of Sesto's words "Guardami, e tutto oblio" (Ex. 28) and his setting of the very first words that Sesto sang in his duet with Vitellia, "Come ti piace imponi" (see Ex. 14 above) suggests that Sesto remains as much as ever under Vitellia's control. His excitement and anxiety is expressed by a further acceleration of tempo, to Allegro assai, with nervous triplets in the clarinet part; Sesto then takes up the triplets in a display of coloratura; breathless rests separate words within phrases ("ah qual . . . poter . . . oh Dei!") and syllables within words ("al . . . la bel . . . tà") as the aria reaches its climax.

Sesto finally goes off to begin the rebellion. As Vitellia gloats over her impending triumph over Tito, Publio and Annio enter and announce to Vitellia that she must go to Tito; he has chosen her to be his wife. The news throws Vitellia into confusion. A trio (G major), dominated by Vitellia's fragmented exclamations, follows; we saw in chapter 3 how Mazzolà crafted the text from blank verse that Metastasio had intended to be set as recitative. Vitellia's first incoherent words –

> Vengo . . . aspettate . . . Sesto! . . .
> Ahime! . . . Sesto! . . . è partito?

> I'm coming . . . wait . . . Sesto! . . . Oh no! . . . Sesto! . . . has he left?

– are presumably meant to be heard by the other characters. What follows is an aside in which Vitellia expresses her anguish and horror to the audience. Her confused state of mind is apparent to Annio and Publio, although they do not understand its cause; they sing together:

> Oh come un gran contento,
> Come confonde un cor.

> How a great happiness confuses a heart.

Scenes 11–14: the Forum

Sesto, alone, expresses his confusion in a long and agitated accompanied recitative whose pathos is enhanced by irony. Sesto struggles to convince himself to do something that he knows is wrong, because that is what Vitellia ordered him to do; as we watch Sesto struggle, we know that Vitellia is desperately looking for him, so that she can tell him to call off the coup. Sesto's excitement is represented in the orchestra by the recurrence of a menacing motive first heard in C minor (Ex. 29). This idea is closely related to the first theme of the overture, with its x and y phrases (see Ex. 9 above); here the staccato eighth-notes of phrase x are combined with syncopated quarter-notes of phrase y.

Remorse enters Sesto's heart as he thinks of the virtue of the sovereign whom he is about to slay. His thoughts are reflected by a gentle melodic line and a turn to the major mode. He decides to withdraw from the conspiracy; but just as he makes this decision a fire breaks out on the Capitol. His change of heart has come too late. The rebellion has begun.

Sesto begins the quintet with chorus that brings Act I to a close (text by Mazzolà). This finale, in E flat major, is the longest and most complex movement in *La clemenza di Tito*. The conspicuous reference to E flat at the beginning of the overture's violent development section sounds, in retrospect, like an adumbration of this climactic scene. Just as the development section is the emotional core of the overture, this finale is the emotional core of *Tito* as a whole.

Sesto prays to the gods, asking them to save Tito. Annio enters, followed by Servilia; at about the same time Sesto disappears into the fray. Excitement increases as the music moves to C minor; we

Ex. 29

realize now that the appearance of C minor at the beginning of Sesto's accompanied recitative foreshadowed the outbreak of the rebellion. The arrival of C minor is accompanied with string tremolos and the sound of trumpets and drums, the effect of whose sudden entrance at this moment is increased by the fact that these instruments have not been heard since the triumphal march much earlier in the act.

An off-stage chorus is suddenly heard crying out on a diminished-seventh chord: "Ah!" Thus the people of Rome express their horror at the violence that has broken out (Ex. 30). The idea of an off-stage chorus making an interjection on a diminished-seventh chord was not new with Mazzolà and Mozart. Lorenzo Da Ponte and Antonio Salieri experimented with the same device four years earlier in one of their most successful operas, *Axur, re d'Ormus* (Vienna, 1788; see Ex. 31). But Mozart makes much more insistent use of his off-stage chorus than Salieri; and he integrates it more effectively into the scene. Tonal instability, syncopations, and abrupt shifts of dynamics all contribute to the sense of confusion and terror. Nowhere in eighteenth-century music has political turmoil been more vividly evoked than in this finale, in which we may be able to hear a musical echo of the revolutionary age that created it.

Sesto enters, announcing that Tito has been killed. When Servilia, Annio and Publio ask who did the deed Sesto is about to confess that he stabbed the emperor, but Vitellia breaks in and

Ex. 30

Salieri, *Axur, re d'Ormus*, Act 1: Duet "Per te solo, amato bene"
Source: Autograph score (Vienna, Nationalbibliothek), Fol. 22v-23r

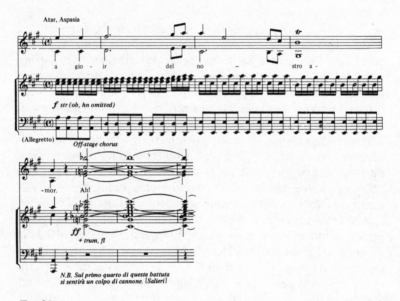

Ex. 31

keeps him quiet. The act ends with a mournful ensemble for soloists and chorus, "Oh nero tradimento." To end an act with a slow movement, an Andante, was very rare in eighteenth-century opera; the effect of this movement is that of a funeral march.

Act II

Scenes 1–4: a secluded garden

The rebellion has been suppressed, and Tito has survived unharmed. When Annio announces these tidings to Sesto, the reluctant rebel expresses his happiness that Tito is alive; he admits his guilt to Annio and tells of his intention to flee from Rome. Annio tries to persuade him to stay, to confess everything to Tito, and to trust in his clemency. Annio expresses the tenderness and warmth of his feelings for both the emperor and Sesto in the gentle aria "Torna di Tito al lato" (text by Mazzolà, G major.)

It is fitting in an aria about Tito that Tito's musical language should be evoked. This aria shares with Tito's "Del più sublime soglio" not only the key of G major and a simple A B A' structure, but also harmonic and melodic details. Both arias move through E minor and D major in their B sections; the beautiful passage cited by Heartz in "Del più sublime soglio" (see Ex. 24 above) finds an echo in Annio's aria (Ex. 32). At the same time the simpler texture and orchestration of Annio's aria (strings alone) remind us that he is a character of secondary importance.

Having assured Sesto of Tito's goodness and urged him to meet with the emperor, Annio leaves the stage. Then Vitellia appears and gives Sesto just the opposite advice: he should flee. She is concerned not so much about Sesto as about her own fortune: she still hopes for the crown; and she is convinced that Sesto, if arrested, will ruin her chances by confessing everything, including her part in the plot, to the emperor. Sesto promises that he will never betray her, but Vitellia has her doubts: she is suspicious of

Ex. 32

virtuous feelings, whether Sesto's love for Tito or Tito's willingness
to forgive:

> Mi fiderei,
> Se minor tenerezza
> Per Tito in te vedessi. Il suo rigore
> Non temo già; la sua clemenza io temo;
> Questa ti vincerà.

> I would be more trusting if I saw in you less tenderness for Tito. I
> do not fear his harshness; I fear his clemency; that will conquer
> you.

They are interrupted by Publio, who demands Sesto's sword and
arrests him, informing him that the man whom he, Sesto, stabbed
was not Tito but the conspirator Lentulo dressed as Tito. Lentulo
has survived the wound and has implicated Sesto in the plot.

In the trio "Se al volto mai ti senti" (text by Mazzolà, B flat
major) we see the feelings of Sesto, Vitellia and Publio evolve. First
Sesto offers Vitellia a plaintive farewell. His melody is gentle and
tonally stable (Ex. 33). Vitellia's entrance, much as in the duet
"Come ti piace imponi" is accompanied by more active rhythms
and tonal instability – here a violent turn to the parallel minor
(Ex. 34); but where in the duet Vitellia expressed indignation and
strength of mind, now she just as vividly expresses shame and

Ex. 33

Ex. 34

Ram - men - ta chi t'a - do - ra in ques - to sta - to an - co - ra

Ex. 35

(L'a - cer - bo a-ma - ro pian - to, che da' suoi lu - mi pio - ve,

l'a - ni-ma mi com - mo - ve, mi com - mo - ve . . .)

Ex. 36

confusion. Publio, at first unmoved by the emotions of Sesto and Vitellia, can only repeat his command that Sesto follow him.

The tempo shifts from Andantino to Allegretto and Sesto sings a sentimental tune (Ex. 35) whose pathos further weakens Vitellia's defenses; her agitation is betrayed by the insistent dotted rhythms that she sings. At this point Publio too is moved to pity: his commands to follow give way finally to lyrical exclamation (Ex. 36).

Scenes 5–15: an audience chamber in the imperial palace

Patricians, praetorians, and people give thanks to the gods for Tito's survival in the chorus "Ah grazie si rendano." The chorus is in the form A B A', with section B sung by Tito himself, as he thanks his subjects for their concern. Tito awaits news of Sesto's trial, certain that his friend will be found innocent. Publio warns him that "not everyone has Tito's heart," and in his only aria, "Tardi s'avvede" (text by Metastasio), he reflects on the tendency of the virtuous to be blind to the faults of others.

Publio leaves, but returns soon after with Annio. The trial is over; Sesto has confessed his guilt; the death sentence awaits only the emperor's signature. Annio begs Tito for mercy (Plate 7); Publio urges him to the amphitheater where the people await; Tito impatiently dismisses both. Before leaving, Annio pleads once more for the life of his friend in the aria "Tu fosti tradito" (text by Mazzolà, F major.)

When Annio has left, Tito launches into the first of his three

7   Diana Montague as Annio and David Rendall as Tito in Jean-Pierre Ponnelle's production at the Metropolitan Opera, 1987

great monologues, two of them set by Mozart as accompanied recitatives, that are among the musical and dramatic highpoints of the opera. Even before Tito speaks, the orchestra expresses his agony at Sesto's betrayal: the strings, *forte*, play a syncopated diminished chord, almost a cry of pain (Ex. 37). We should

Ex. 37

recognize this chord: Mozart planted it in two prominent places in the overture, near the end of the exposition and near the end of the development section. Tito picks up the pen to sign the death sentence; but then he stops, deciding that he must first give Sesto a chance to explain his actions. As he waits for Sesto to appear, the emperor reflects once again on the hardships of his state; a poor peasant is more fortunate than a king. Tito meditates on the simple life of country folk in a passage full of dreamy lyricism. At the moment when his thoughts shift from the peasant's life to his own –

> Noi, fra tante grandezze,
> Sempre incerti viviam . . .
>
> We, amidst such grandeur, live in constant uncertainty . . .

– Mozart switches from a gentle accompaniment of strings to more prosaic simple recitative; the next few bars of simple recitative are the only ones in *La clemenza di Tito* that survive in Mozart's hand, evidence that the idea of using the transition from accompanied to simple recitative as a dramatic device was Mozart's own.

Publio arrives, and then Sesto. In the trio "Quello di Tito è il volto" (E flat major), fashioned by Mazzolà and Mozart out of a long series of asides in Metastasio's recitative, Sesto, Tito, and Publio express their feelings. Sesto is surprised and frightened by Tito's harsh expression; fluttering thirty-second-notes in the orchestra depict his trembling. Tito finds Sesto's remorseful expression equally surprising; his lyrical melody, in contrast to his stern countenance, seems to express pity rather than anger. Publio comments on the conflicting feelings that struggle within Tito.

Publio leaves Tito and Sesto alone. The scene that follows was one of the most famous and admired in all of Metastasio's dramas during the eighteenth century. Voltaire, in the preface to his tragedy *Sémiramis*, pointed to this scene and the soliloquy for Tito that follows as pinnacles of Metastasio's dramatic art, "comparable to the finest that Greece ever produced, if not superior ... worthy of Corneille when he is not making speeches, and of Racine when he is not weak ... based not on operatic love but on the noble sentiments of the human heart.'

Except for the last few lines of recitative, from which Mazzolà fashioned a new exit-aria for Sesto, Mozart let Metastasio's dialogue stand as he wrote it, completely uncut, and he allowed it to be set in simple recitative, presumably in the belief that Metastasio's scene was dramatically effective as the poet envisaged it. Yet today the scene is usually performed with extensive cuts. Directors and performers apparently fear that listeners will be bored by the long stretch of simple recitative. Even an enthusiastic admirer of *Tito* like the Canadian musicologist Don J. Neville finds this scene too long, too dull.[8] Certainly from a purely musical point of view this scene, like other scenes declaimed in simple recitative, has little to offer. But that is one of the points of simple recitative, as was argued in chapter 2: Mozart wanted audiences to hear Metastasio's poetry, to be moved by Metastasio's dramatic situation as communicated not so much through singing as through acting. To appreciate this scene, to understand why Mazzolà and Mozart made it part of their opera, we have to consider Metastasio's text as it might be presented on stage by two great actors who are convinced that they are presenting one of the opera's most important scenes.

The emperor, moved by Sesto's dejected expression, addresses him with kindness, asking him if it is really true that Sesto has betrayed both his friend and his emperor. Tito seems hardly to be able to believe what has happened. He can do nothing but ask questions – eight in a row, without stopping for an answer. Tito is hurt, disappointed, but not angry. His questions are full of comforting words – *padre* (father), *benefattor* (benefactor), *amico* (friend), *tenera cura* (tender care).

Sesto falls on his knees, overcome with remorse. More impulsive than Tito, he interrupts the emperor in mid-verse, begging to be punished for his crime. His speech is a self-accusation, answering Tito's positive words with negative ones: *misero cor* (wretched heart), *spergiuro* (perjured), *ingrato* (ingrate), *colpe mie* (my crimes), *soffrir* (to suffer), *supplizio* (torture), *morir* (to die), *infedel* (unfaithful), *perfido sangue* (perfidious blood). Sesto's unstable state of mind is expressed by frequent repetition: *Non più, non più*; *Tutte ... tutte ... tutti*; *Affretta ... affretta ...* By having Sesto use the words *clementissimo* and *clemenza* in reference to Tito, Metastasio isolates this speech as a crucial one within the context of the whole opera, a speech in which the tragedy of Sesto's betrayal is given its most intense expression.

Tito, pitying Sesto, orders him to rise and to explain why he committed such a crime. In words quoted admiringly by Voltaire, Tito asks Sesto to confide in him as a friend; if Sesto does, perhaps Tito might be able to find some way to pardon him:

> Odimi, o Sesto:
> Siam soli; il tuo sovrano
> Non è presente. Apri il tuo core a Tito,
> Confidati all'amico; io ti prometto
> Che Augusto nol saprà. Del tuo delitto
> Dì la prima cagion. Cerchiamo insieme
> Una via di scusarti. Io ne sarei
> Forse di te più lieto.

> Listen to me, Sesto. We are alone; your sovereign is not here. Open your heart to your friend; I promise that Augustus [i.e. the emperor] will not know. Tell me the real reason why you committed this crime. Let us find a way to pardon you. Perhaps I should be happier about it than you.

Sesto faces the agonizing choice of lying to his friend or betraying the woman he loves. As Tito's appeals become increasingly emotional, Sesto becomes increasingly desperate. The rising intensity of emotion is reflected in shorter and shorter speeches, until each says only a few words before stopping, sometimes in mid-sentence, or being interrupted by the other. Sesto finally breaks down, calling himself a traitor and asking resolutely for death. Tito simultaneously reaches the end of his patience. Having pleaded unsuccessfully, having had his clemency thrown back at him, Tito is overcome by anger. He promises Sesto that death is what he will indeed have, if he wants it; and he calls in the guards to take Sesto away. Sesto begs to be allowed to kiss Tito's hand for the last time, and this request leads him to the culmination of the scene, the rondò "Deh per questo istante solo."

The recitative, quite apart from its own dramatic merits, affects the way we hear the aria that follows. With its constantly shifting tonal centers, its bare sonority, its strictly limited melodic, rhythmic, and harmonic vocabulary, the recitative both serves as a break from the musical richness of the trio "Quello di Tito è il volto" and builds up expectation for the following number. When performed quite rapidly, the entire confrontation of Sesto and Tito takes about four minutes. Thus we know that Mozart intended the end of the trio "Quello di Tito è il volto" to be separated by at least four minutes from Sesto's rondò. The perfect sense of theatrical timing that Mozart exhibited in his Viennese operas did not desert him here. The beautiful Adagio melody with which "Deh per questo istante solo" begins takes on unexpected freshness, and unexpected pathos, when it is performed after a long and emotional scene in which audiences hear no tonal stability, no lyrical melody, and no orchestra.

"Deh per questo istante solo" (text by Mazzolà, A major), like Vitellia's "Non più di fiori," is a two-tempo rondò, a particular type of aria defined both by its form and its function in late eighteenth-century opera. Rondòs were normally granted only to the *primo uomo* and *prima donna* as vehicles for the display of their virtuosity and expressivity. Librettists often placed rondòs near the end of the opera, and audiences looked forward to them as musical and dramatic high-points of their theatrical experience.

The rondò, both poetry and music, was subject to rigid conventions. The typical rondò is a setting of a poem of twelve *ottonari* (eight- and sometimes seven-syllable lines) arranged in three quatrains. The rondò consists of two sections, the first slow and the second fast; these two sections are often linked by a transition passage in either the slow tempo or the fast.

The slow section of the typical rondò is in the form A B A. It begins with a setting of the first quatrain as a lyrical melody (A) in duple meter. Contrasting material follows: the second quatrain set in a more dramatic, more declamatory style (B). Then the opening melody is repeated. The transition passage, if there is one, often leads to an open cadence on the dominant. The fast section, also in duple meter, consists of another melody in the tonic (often a setting of the last two lines of text) presented two or three times in alternation with contrasting episodes, followed by closing material.

"Deh per questo istante solo" follows most of these conventions. The opening slow melody is just the kind of gentle, melancholy tune that one would expect in a rondò (Ex. 38). It is followed by contrasting material which culminates in a passage of extraordinary harmonic richness and expressive intensity; this leads, as we expect, to the return of the opening melody.

Bedini's long experience as a *primo uomo* in Italy may be

Deh per que - sto i - stan - te so - lo   ti   ri - cor - da il   pri - mo a - mor.

Ex. 38

reflected in an unusual feature of this rondò: unusual, that is, in the context of Mozart's *œuvre*. The slow section of many Italian rondòs ends with a literal repetition of the opening melody A. That, at any rate, is how it appears on paper. In performance the virtuoso performing the rondò was expected to ornament the melody elaborately and tastefully on its return; no two performances by a first-rate *prima donna* or *primo uomo* of a rondò melody would sound exactly the same. Mozart's rondòs differ from the Italian norm in that he rarely brought back melody A of the slow section unchanged. He typically varied the accompaniment in some attractive way. For example, in the rondò "Al desio di chi t'adora," a replacement aria he wrote for *Le nozze di Figaro* in 1789, the second appearance of melody A has a new accompaniment of pizzicato strings; and when melody A returns in Fiordiligi's rondò "Per pietà ben mio perdona," the opening words, originally accompanied by strings, are now accompanied by two horns. The effect of these changes is to take the audience's attention away from the singer, at least momentarily; and they discourage the singer from adding his or her own ornamentation.

Mozart had plenty of experience in the composing of rondòs by the time he came to compose *La clemenza di Tito*. But he had never written a rondò for a *musico*. This is perhaps why, when he wrote his rondò for Bedini, he departed from his normal practice. The opening material returns completely unchanged. Bedini may have insisted on keeping for himself the privilege of ornamenting his melody. In any case Mozart, under pressure of time, had the good sense to entrust this important aspect of performance to his talented and experienced singer.

The slow section is followed by a shift in tempo to Allegro and a transitional passage that the listener familiar with the conventions of the rondò expects to be followed by a new melody in A major, the tonic. But instead we move quickly away from the tonic, and Sesto enters suddenly in C major on the words "Disperato vado a morte." There is something recklessly heroic about this moment – C major, which we associate with the grandeur and celebration of

(Tan - to af - fan - no sof - fre un co - re, nè si mo - re di do - lor. . .)

Ex. 39

the overture, appearing so suddenly in such tragic circumstances. And this is not the only sudden modulation by a third in this aria: later in the aria Mozart moves with equally dramatic effect from A major to F major.

Mozart regains A major and presents the principal theme of the fast section (Ex. 39). This melody has been subject to much criticism, especially in the nineteenth century. The great Mozart scholar Otto Jahn, for example, dismissed it as "too soft and tender." We can see what he objected too. But in fact softness and tenderness is exactly what eighteenth-century listeners wanted in this context. In order to appreciate this melody we have to try to hear it as they did.

Eighteenth-century audiences expected a rondò to be not deeply tragic, but touching, not intensely expressive, but delicate and sentimental. Such a rondò, performed by a great singer, could bring an audience to tears. Here is how one listener, an Italian poet, responded to a rondò in 1780, as sung by the male soprano Luigi Marchesi at La Scala:

Ah! I feel it here . . . here in my heart, always delightful, always varied; [his voice] opens for me new, unimagined and unimaginable sources of sweetness . . . I do not remember anything else; the whole of nature was nothing for me in that moment; an indefinable spell of pleasure, of voluptuousness, penetrates my senses, puts reason to sleep. All my senses are concentrated on this heavenly song . . . my heart swells . . . I cannot resist the flood of delight that inundates me . . . sighs issue forth in a crowd; I end with sobs, with tears, and with applause. The whole theater responds to my sensibility; all the audience is engulfed in the same delightful delirium.[9]

The rondò with which Marchesi reduced his audience to such tearful ecstasy was Giuseppe Sarti's "Mia speranza io pur vorrei," an aria in A major. Sesto's A-major rondò "Deh per questo istante solo" has much the same structure, sound and spirit as Sarti's. There is no reason why it could not be as effective in the theater. Performed by a soprano who can bring Sesto's words and feelings vividly to life and can ornament the vocal line spontaneously and beautifully, and heard by an audience that is willing to be moved by the music's delicate sweetness and the singer's emotional expression, "Deh per questo istante solo" could represent musical drama at its most intense and memorable.

After Sesto has been led away by the guards, Tito angrily walks to the table where the death sentence awaits his signature. Here begins his second soliloquy. In ordering Sesto's death, he says, his neglected, despised clemency will gain its revenge. But at the word "vendetta" Tito stops, surprised that such a thought has occurred to him. He thinks for a moment of pardon, but then considers that he should not ignore the law. He is resolute:

> Sesto è reo: Sesto mora.

> Sesto is guilty: Sesto shall die.

He signs the death warrant. But Tito cannot suppress for long his feelings of generosity; and he thinks of his reputation too:

> Or che diranno
> I posteri di noi? Diran che in Tito
> Si stancò la clemenza.

> Now what will future generations say of us? They will say that in Tito clemency grew tired.

Tito finally gives in to his generous nature; he tears up the paper and, as he throws away the pieces, he concludes grandly that if the world is to accuse him of some mistake, it is better to be accused of mercy than of harshness.

Clemency has triumphed, but only the audience and Tito know. During the next few scenes all the other characters speak and act in the belief that Tito has in fact signed the death sentence. This misunderstanding gives the last part of Mozart's opera a delicate layer of irony that contributes to its extraordinary pathos.

Publio enters; the emperor tells him that Sesto's fate has been decided. In an aside ("Oh sventurato!") Publio expresses his pity for the prisoner who, he believes, is about to die. But Tito, in his last and finest aria, "Se all'impero" (text by Metastasio; B flat major), which must likewise be an aside to the audience that shares his secret, rejoices in his decision to pardon Sesto.

The enlightened monarch represents tradition; that is surely one reason why Mazzolà and Mozart made a point of giving Tito original, Metastasian aria-texts for all three of his arias. Mozart may have been making a similar point when he adopted a structure for "Se all'impero" that looks back to the da capo aria of the

baroque and early classical periods. This is not a da capo aria, but
one in which the three-part da capo form, A B A, is modified
under the influence of sonata form. The opening A section,
analogous to the exposition in sonata form, modulates from tonic to
dominant; the tonally unstable B section is analogous to the
development in sonata form; and the concluding section, A', in the
tonic throughout, is analogous to the recapitulation.

One must hear "Se all'impero" in context, with the joyful opening
ritornello directly following, and contradicting, the mournful
Publio's aside 'Oh sventurato!' A rich complement of woodwinds
(pairs of flutes, oboes, and bassoons) together with a pair of high-
pitched horns in B flat *alto* – at eight instruments this is the largest
orchestral wind ensemble in any aria in *La clemenza di Tito* – gives
Mozart's orchestra a brilliant sonority. Repeated eighth-notes in the
bass and a pattern of syncopated quarter-notes in the second violins
contribute to the music's exhilarating rhythmic vitality (Ex. 40).

Just as the juxtaposition of Publio's 'Oh sventurato!' and the
beginning of "Se all'impero" enhances the joyfulness of the aria's
opening ritornello, so the A and A' sections serve as a dramatic foil
to the pathos of the B section. The tempo slows from allegro to
andantino; the meter switches from duple to triple; the orchestra,
to begin with, is limited to strings alone, *piano*. Tito sings an
eight-measure lyrical melody: this is late Mozart at his most *dolce*
(Ex. 41). But when Tito reaches the words

> D'una fede non mi curo
> Che sia frutto del timor

> I have no interest in a fidelity that is the fruit of fear

the emotional temperature begins to rise, with the introduction first
of arpeggiation in staccato eighth-notes in the first violins and
syncopated quarter-notes in the seconds; then, in the following
measure, the turn to diminished-seventh harmony. A sudden

Ex. 40

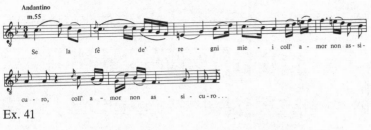

Ex. 41

Ex. 42

feeling of tragedy intensifies as the arpeggiation in staccato eighth-notes is transformed into sixteenth-notes and the horns enter, playing a dominant pedal in octaves that has a menacing quality in this context (Ex. 42).

Tito can feel and express both the depths of human tragedy and the heights of human greatness; he touches tragedy in the B section of "Se all'impero"; he reaches greatness in the climactic display of coloratura in the A' section (see Ex. 4 above). So many tenors have come to grief on this coloratura that some may have been tempted to take up Andrew Porter's suggestion "to simplify the all but unsingable bars . . . rather than smudge them in a brave attempt."[10]

Ex. 43

But let us hope that tenors continue their brave attempts: for it is the audacious, almost superhuman exuberance of this coloratura that more than anything else conveys Tito's sense of triumph at this crucial point in the opera.

The emperor is finally reconciled to his role as sovereign. Instead of feeling his duties only as torments that he must bear, he can rejoice in his power, in his *impero*. The sudden turn to G minor near the end of the aria – one of several ideas that Mozart seems to have remembered from Ottavio's "Il mio tesoro" when he wrote again for Antonio Baglioni in 1791 (see Exx. 6 and 7) – leads to a coda-like declaration of Tito's credo as the winds once again take up the *"impero*-motive" (compare Ex. 43 to Exx. 21 and 27). Baglioni influenced the composition of this aria by making it possible for Mozart to return to melodic, harmonic, and orchestrational ideas that he had successfully applied to an aria written for the same singer several years earlier. Yet the *"impero*-motive" is very much part of *La clemenza di Tito*. For all its similarities to the earlier aria, "Se all'impero" is very different from it. "Il mio tesoro" is a lyrical love song, tender and intimate. "Se all'impero" is a public declaration: a victorious celebration of the human spirit.

Tito departs for the arena. Vitellia appears and, when Publio cannot tell her what Sesto has said to Tito, she assumes that Sesto has told of her part in the conspiracy. She resolves to confess all to the emperor; but then Servilia and Annio enter and ask her to intercede with the emperor on Sesto's behalf: only Vitellia, as Tito's bride, can move him to rescind the death sentence. Thus Vitellia learns, to her amazement, that Sesto has not betrayed her.

> Dunque Sesto ha taciuto! Oh amore! Oh fede!

> So Sesto has kept silent! What love! What faithfulness!

Vitellia is moved; she cannot decide what to do; she refuses to come with Annio and Servilia; she says she will follow after them; she weeps, and Servilia tells her, in the tender little aria "S'altro che lacrime" (text by Metastasio, A major) that tears alone will not help Sesto.

Left alone, Vitellia faces the consequences of her recklessness. This is her first and only soliloquy, the first and only time in the opera that she has been forced to face herself, to wrestle with her feelings. She must finally feel some of the agony of indecision that she has forced Sesto to feel. Her pity for Sesto, about to die on account of a crime committed at her command, her remorse and her fear put Vitellia in a state of turmoil; she sees clearly only one thing: that she must confess her part in the rebellion, even though that will mean giving up what she wants most of all:

> A' piedi suoi vadasi
> Il tutto a palesar.
> Si scemi il delitto di Sesto,
> Se scusar non si può, col fallo mio.
> D'impero e d'imenei, speranze, addio.

> Let me go and confess all at his feet. Let Sesto's crime, if it cannot be forgiven, be lessened through my guilt. Farewell, hopes of empire and marriage!

Vitellia's rondò with obbligato basset horn, "Non più di fiori larghe catene," "No more long chains of flowers" (author of text unknown, possibly Mazzolà, F major), has some unusual features. The poem has the twelve lines that one expects in a rondò poem, but the first two quatrains consist of very short *quinari* (five-syllable lines) rather than the normal *ottonari*. Only the third and final quatrain uses *ottonari*. The *quinari* have a strongly dactylic quality: Nón più di fíori / Lárghe caténe. They invite a musical setting in triple meter. That helps to explain another unusual aspect of this rondò: the slow section is in triple meter, rather than the duple meter that is almost universal in rondòs. Mozart had a precedent for such a departure from convention close at hand. Martín y Soler's celebrated comic opera *L'arbore di Diana* (Vienna, 1787) has a rondò that begins in triple meter, "Teco porta, o mia speranza." Martín's F-major rondò, like Mozart's, moves from a triple-meter slow section to a duple-meter fast section, and presents within the fast section a speeded-up, duple-meter version of the slow melody. Mozart must have known "Teco porta, o mia speranza"; it may well have served as inspiration for "Non più di fiori."

Ex. 44

Vitellia's rondò begins with the section in slow tempo and A B A form that we expect in a rondò. A gentle melody is presented first by the violins, with Anton Stadler's basset horn part doubling the melody an octave lower. When Vitellia enters (Ex. 44), the basset horn is silent; but when melody A is repeated the basset horn accompanies it with triplet arpeggiation (a good example of Mozart's tendency to vary melody A when it recurs in his rondòs). Vitellia's opening Larghetto is much shorter than the opening slow section of most rondòs. This brevity finds compensation in the extraordinary expansion, both musical and emotional, of the following fast section, in which fear, despair, and self-pity succeed one another in a musical and dramatic tour-de-force that the American musicologist James Parakilas has perceptively analyzed as a mad-scene.[11] The aria's final orchestral *tutti* leads directly into a transition passage that accompanies a change of scene.

Scenes 16–17: an amphitheater

The transition passage is brief – seven measures – and intensely dramatic. It begins with a sudden shift of tempo from Allegro to Andante maestoso. Simultaneously the trumpets and drums, heard for the first time in Act II, enter with dotted rhythms. We move quickly through the circle of fifths from F to C to G, and the transition concludes, like a similar passage in the second-act finale of Salieri's *Axur, re d'Ormus*, on a grand open cadence. This is a splendid moment. From the private agony of Vitellia we are brought with brilliant suddenness into the public grandeur of a magnificent amphitheater, and the people of Rome praise Tito in the great chorus "Che del ciel, che degli dei" (text by Metastasio; G major).

Tito asks for Sesto to be brought before him; Annio and Servilia make a final plea for mercy (Plate 8). The emperor addresses Sesto, numbers his offences, and is about to announce his pardon when Vitellia rushes in. To the amazement of all she confesses her part in the rebellion. Tito, in his third and final monologue, expresses his frustration and indignation:

8   Act II, Scene 16 in Jean-Pierre Ponnelle's production at the
Metropolitan Opera, 1987

> Ma che giorno è mai questo?
> Al punto stesso che assolvo un reo,
> Ne scopro un altro?

> What kind of day is this? On the point of forgiving one criminal I
> discover another?

His anger turns to yearning as he asks the gods, after a modulation
of exquisite beauty from harsh A minor to gentle F major, if he will
ever find a faithful soul (Ex. 45). Again Tito is tempted to give way
to vengeance; again he decides quickly that his generous instincts
will triumph. He commands that Sesto and his fellow conspirators
be freed; like his first words in Act I, Tito's final pronouncement
(derived from the last lines of Corneille's *Cinna, ou la clémence
d'Auguste*) is a maxim of enlightened absolutism:

> Sia noto a Roma
> Ch'io son lo stesso, e ch'io
> Tutto so, tutti assolvo, e tutto oblio.

> Let it be known to Rome that I have not changed, that I know all,
> forgive all, and forget all.

Ex. 45

Ex. 46

The tonal destination of Tito's monologue is C major. The arrival of C major completes a tonal progression on a grand scale. The subdominant-dominant-tonic progression represented by "Non più di fiori" (F), "Che del ciel" (G) and the final, triumphant ensemble with chorus, "Tu, è ver, m'assolvi, Augusto" (text by Mazzolà, C major), mirrors the one linking the opera's overture and the first three vocal numbers. The ensemble gradually builds in strength. As in the first-act quintet with chorus, Mozart withholds the chorus, as well as the trumpets and drums, until an important point later in the movement. The key of C major brings us back to the festive realm of the overture, as does the orchestration. The orchestra's final unison slides, from the fifth scale degree up to the tonic, bring the opera to a close with the same gesture as that with which it began (compare Ex. 46 to Ex. 8). Thus the stability and strength evoked by the beginning of the overture is reaffirmed by the opera's final chords.

6   Tito *in performance, 1791–1850*

During the half-decade following the premiere of *La clemenza di Tito* in Prague the opera was not performed often, but it slowly became better known after 1795. *Tito* was the first of Mozart's operas to be performed in London, in 1806. The following year it reached Naples; in 1816 it was performed in Paris, in 1817 in both Milan and St. Petersburg. By 1815 *Tito* was a familiar item in the repertory of many German theaters and those of Prague, Vienna, and London (the only city outside of central Europe where it held the stage for more than a few isolated performances.) Interest in *Tito* gradually diminished after 1820, as it evolved from a standard of the German operatic repertory to an opera only occasionally, and usually unsuccessfully, revived. By the time Edward Dent published *Mozart's operas* (1913), *Tito* was "little suited to modern conditions"; in the second edition (1947) Dent could dismiss the opera even more emphatically: "For the stage of today it can only be considered as a museum piece."[1]

The rise and fall of *Tito* during the first half of the nineteenth century suggest many questions. Why was the opera staged so rarely in the years immediately following the premiere? What caused the rapid increase in productions around 1800? What was it about productions of *Tito* during the early nineteenth century, not only in Germany but in Prague, Vienna, and London, that made many of them so successful? Why did interest in *Tito* begin to wane in the 1820s and 1830s?

Constanze Mozart as champion of *Tito*

News of the unsuccessful premiere of *Tito* spread quickly. An article in the *Musikalisches Wochenblatt* of Berlin concerning musical events at the Prague coronation called *La clemenza di Tito* "a grand – or rather a middle-sized – serious opera," and went on to

104

criticize Mozart for having composed too quickly: "This otherwise great composer seems this time to have forgotten the motto of Octavius, 'Festina lente!' Furthermore, only the arias and choruses were by his hand; the recitatives were by another."[2] This report and others like it may have contributed to a less than enthusiastic interest in *Tito* during the years following its premiere. *Tito* was performed rarely if at all during 1792 and 1793; during those same years *Die Zauberflöte* was produced in at least sixteen different cities.[3]

Constanze Mozart was *Tito*'s first promoter. Between 1794 and 1797 she organized a series of concerts and concert tours featuring Mozart's music in order to raise money for herself and her children. She seems to have taken a personal interest in *Tito* and to have depended on it as a special part of her programs, often performing one of the roles herself. On some occasions she presented the whole score (but probably not including simple recitative) in concert performance.

Typical of Constanze Mozart's efforts to promote *Tito* is this advertisement for a concert performance of the opera in Vienna in December 1794:

The Imperial Royal High Court Theater Direction has graciously permitted the undersigned to give a concert for her benefit during the present Advent season. She has selected for this occasion one of the best and last works of her husband, who died too early for her and for art, the late Imperial Royal Court Chamber Composer Wolfgang Amadé Mozart, namely the music that he wrote for Metastasio's opera *La clemenza di Tito*, music that has not yet been performed here. The universal applause with which Mozart's musical products were always received encourages her to hope that the respected Public will honor with its presence the performance of one of his last masterpieces. The day of the performance of this music, and the names of the singers, will be made known in due course by means of the usual posters.

Mozart, née Weber[4]

The concert must have been successful, for Mozart's widow continued to use *Tito* in her benefit concerts. In September 1795 she and her son Karl gave a concert in Graz; there again *Tito* was on the program, advertised as Mozart's last work, "a masterpiece completely unknown except in Vienna and Prague."[5] Soon thereafter she went on a concert tour through Germany with her sister Aloisia Lange. Their concert at the Gewandhaus in Leipzig was dominated by excerpts from *Tito*, as we can see from the program:

Symphony.
Aria *Nò, che non sei capace* [Mozart's K. 419] (Mad. Lange).
Concerto on the Pianoforte (Kapellmeister Eberl).
Terzetto from "Clemenza di Tito" *Vengo, aspettate* (Mad. Mozart, Mad. Lange and Hr. Richter).
March from the same opera.
An Allegro movement.
Recitative and Rondo *Mia speranza adorata* [Mozart's K. 416] (Mad. Lange).
Quartet on the Pianoforte (Eberl).
Duet from "Clemenza di Tito" *Come ti piace, imponi* (Mad. Lange and Mad. Mozart).
Recitative, Quintet, and Chorus from "Clemenza di Tito" *Oh Dei, che smania è questa.*[6]

In February 1796 Constanze Mozart gave a benefit concert in the Royal Opera House in Berlin; and there again excerpts from *Tito* figured prominently on the program.[7] The concert that she organized in Linz in November 1796 consisted almost entirely of excerpts from *Tito*.[8] A year later, in November 1797, she gave a concert in Prague of music that she described in a poster as still completely unknown there. But that was not the case with the music that concluded the program, a chorus from *La clemenza di Tito* to which new words, in celebration of "the joyful return of peace," had been adapted by August Gottlieb Meissner. The program explained that the chorus had been chosen in the hope that the audience might join in the performance; the implication seems to be that the audience was familiar with the music.[9]

Constanze Mozart's concert in Prague was one of the last that she organized. Soon after she gave up her concert tours *Tito* began to be performed on the operatic stage with increasing frequency. Between 1798 and 1801 there were at least twelve productions of *Tito* in Germany and Austria.[10] Appreciation of its musical beauties and dramatic power spread quickly, and performances in many of Europe's operatic centers during the subsequent years made *Tito* one of the best-known of Mozart's operas.

This appreciation grew in spite of, rather than because of Constanze Mozart's promotion of the opera. By insistently referring to *Tito* as one of her husband's last works, Mozart's widow no doubt hoped to endow *Tito* with a special aura that would draw music-lovers to her concerts. By performing the opera as a concert piece she encouraged audiences to think of it as a kind of oratorio, a counterpart to the Requiem among Mozart's last works. Such tactics may have helped her to fill concert halls. But they may also have had the effect of discouraging opera directors, singers, and audiences from thinking of *Tito* as an opera that might work well on stage.

A staple of the repertory in Germany, Austria, and Bohemia, 1800–1820

During the two decades between 1800 and 1820 *La clemenza di Tito* enjoyed a prominent place in the operatic repertory in much of central Europe. The years 1815 to 1817 represented perhaps the height of *Tito*'s popularity; during those years the opera was performed not only in several German cities but also in Vienna, Milan, St. Petersburg, Paris, and London.

1815	Berlin (in German)
	Dresden (in Italian)
1816	Dresden (in Italian)
	Königsberg (in German)
	Berlin (in German)
	London (in Italian)
	Paris (in Italian)
	Stuttgart (in German)
1817	Milan (in Italian)
	Dresden (in Italian)
	Vienna (in German)
	St. Petersburg (in Russian)
	London (in Italian)

The *Allgemeine musikalische Zeitung* of Leipzig, which began publication in 1798, contains many reviews of early nineteenth-century performances of *Tito*. These reviews can help us to understand the values that led to the proliferation of performances of *Tito* in central Europe and that helped to shape them as well. An enthusiasm for great singing was one of these values. Many of Germany's leading singers, including Wilhelmine Schröder-Devrient (who made a specialty of the role of Sesto), took the principal roles of *Tito*. The opera was appreciated for the many opportunities it offered to great singers to display their vocal artistry. But singing was only part of what concerned critics of these performances. Also important for them were staging, costumes, scenery, clear declamation, and expressive acting.

Critics repeatedly expressed a concern for acting. One scolded a tenor for performing a "wooden" Tito in Prague in 1809. Another took a young, inexperienced soprano to task for presenting "the passionate, fiery, stormy Vitellia with too little strength and conviction" in Vienna in 1804. And a third found fault with a soprano whose performance of the role of Sesto in Dresden in 1814 lacked sufficient "passion and youthful impetuousness" and whose delivery of the text should have been more distinct. Indeed the acting of *Tito* seems at times to have interested critics more than the singing. After praising the performances of Vitellia and Sesto in Leipzig during the season 1808–9, a critic asked:

But how can one assign the role of the emperor, at the center of everything, with consideration for nothing other than his not very important arias? That amounts to sacrificing not only that skillful singer, but also the total effect of the work![11]

Evidently this Tito could not act. We might disagree with the reviewer about the importance of Tito's arias. But the comment is of interest in its concern for skills and qualities other than vocal ability.

Several reviews emphasized the importance that early nineteenth-century audiences placed on a clear understanding of *Tito*'s plot as it unfolded. To understand the plot one needed to understand the simple recitative; in order to be understood the recitative had to be declaimed clearly and expressively. Thus praise for the performance of recitative is common in reviews of successful performances of *Tito*. For example, when the opera was first staged at the Court Theater in Vienna, in 1804, Marianna Sessi won compliments for her performance in the role of Sesto, not only in arias but also in recitative: "Marianne Sessi has truly remarkable brilliance and, especially in the higher notes, outstanding power, refinement, and timbre ... She performs difficult and expressive recitatives in an often masterly fashion."[12]

Unfortunately not all performers of *Tito* were as skillful as the Italian Sessi in the performance of recitative. When this Viennese production of *Tito* began to lose audiences, a reviewer blamed ineffective delivery of recitative:

It is difficult to understand why this opera, which a few years ago was seen often and with pleasure at the Theater an der Wien, won so little applause and such small audiences at the Court Theater, if we do not seek the cause in the often unfortunate casting and in the incomprehensibly delivered recitative, which makes it difficult for the listener to understand the drama as a whole. True, Italian operas all have recitative; but the Italian singer takes great pains to pronounce each word clearly, while most German singers consider this kind of music a matter of secondary importance, and believe that they have done everything if they sing well their arias, duets, etc.[13]

The Court Theater found a solution not in cutting the recitative and presenting the opera as a meaningless succession of arias and ensembles, but in translating the opera into German and presenting the recitative as spoken dialogue. Thus *La clemenza di Tito* became *Titus der Grossmütige* (Titus the magnanimous), *Titus der Gütige* (Titus the good), or simply *Titus*. This is how the opera was performed at the Court Theater in Vienna from 1811 and throughout most of Germany during the early nineteenth century. The popularity of *Tito* in German translation and with spoken dialogue is further evidence that German-speaking audiences judged the opera for the way it was acted as well as sung.

Another indication of the value that early nineteenth-century audiences placed on acting was their willingness to permit some of Mozart's arias to be replaced with arias by other composers, if the replacements allowed skillful and committed actors to take roles that they would not otherwise have been able to sing. This was the case, for example, when *Tito* was performed at the Court Theater in Vienna in 1804, with the baritone Antonio Brizzi in the title role. A review of the production mentioned the fact that Brizzi, unable to sing Mozart's tenor arias, replaced them with arias by Joseph Weigl and Simone Mayr; it went on to praise Brizzi's acting, almost as if this had earned him the right to alter Mozart's score:

Because Herr Brizzi has only a baritone voice and not a real tenor, the arias of Titus had to be replaced with new ones, one by Joseph Weigl, the other, connected to a chorus, by Meyer. Brizzi has a beautiful lower register and is very strong both of voice and of execution; his acting, especially in heroic situations, is noble, expressive and perfectly suited to the character he is performing.[14]

Brizzi returned to the role of Tito twelve years later, when the opera was performed in Dresden; and again his performance included arias by Weigl and Mayr.[15]

Another non-tenor who took over the role of Tito was the bass Ludwig Fischer the younger, son of the more famous Ludwig Fischer who created, among many other roles, that of Osmin in Mozart's *Die Entführung aus dem Serail*. Fischer sang the role of Titus in Berlin and Breslau in 1810. Like his father, Fischer was a bass; like Brizzi, he seems to have earned permission to replace Tito's arias (reluctant permission, in the case of this reviewer) by making use of his exceptional ability as an actor:

But certainly Herr Fischer's Titus was very different from Mozart's, and instead of arias not appropriate for his voice, even with its extensive range, he incorporated compositions by Paer and others, which, although they were good in themselves, did not fit in well with Mozart's music. Herr Fischer's acting and declamation were powerful.[16]

Another common feature of performances of *Tito* during the early nineteenth century was the performance of the role of Sesto by tenors. This gave rise to a conflict between those who objected to soprano Sestos on the grounds of dramatic realism (the idea that a soprano hero was unnatural was expressed by influential nineteenth-century critics of *Tito*, as we shall see in chapter 7) and those who saw that transposing Sesto's role damaged the voice-leading in the ensembles in which Sesto takes part. The conflict was discussed in a review of a performance of *Tito* in Prague in 1809; the reviewer chastised the music-director, Wenzel Müller, for allowing the transposition:

Hr. Grünbaum, who put great effort into his portrayal of Sesto, truly outdid himself; but the wish was expressed, and not without reason, that a good soprano return to this role, since that is what ears have grown accustomed to in Prague. It is nothing new that an unmusical stage director should overlook the fact that this kind of transposition destroys the proper relationship between the voices. But that a music director too should say nothing against such an arrangement is not so easy to forgive; one perhaps can only explain the problem to Hr. Wenzel Müller.[17]

Early nineteenth-century critics appreciated the importance to the drama of scenery and costumes as well as acting; they commented on the performance of the chorus as well as that of the soloists. A lavish production of *Tito* in Frankfurt in 1799 won praise in the *Allgemeine musikalische Zeitung* for having brought every element together into a perfect whole (*vollkommnes Ganze*) unrivalled by previous operatic productions in Frankfurt. The critic twice used the word *Pracht* (majesty, splendor), as if this particular quality played some special role in the production.

So finally Titus was given here recently for the first time. The value of this opera and Mozart's immortal name are too obvious for me to have anything to say on the subject; it was enough that everything competed to make itself worthy of the honor of performing this work.

The splendor with which this opera was given surpassed everyone's expectations, including mine. Remarkable was the phenomenon, normally

9   Giorgio Fuentes, stage design, probably for the production of *Tito* in Frankfurt, 1799

so rare, of taste and splendor going hand in hand. Scenery, costumes, props; everything, in short, down to the smallest detail was planned and executed with the greatest accuracy after ancient Roman models. One needed only to pay attention to find oneself transported to ancient Rome.

The music, at least in hindsight, went perfectly, in that not even the smallest mistake occurred. Certainly it happened, as in any theater, that some roles could have been better cast. The choruses were performed with outstanding precision. The singers who pleased most were Herr Schulz as Titus and Madame Cannabich as Sextus; Madame Heinemann too received merited applause in the role of Vitellia. Everyone agrees that no one has seen in Frankfurt such a perfect whole.[18]

The scenery for this production was designed by Giorgio Fuentes, formerly scenic designer at La Scala. His scenery for *Tito* impressed Goethe's mother, who wrote that the rendering of the Capitol was so splendid (*prächtig*) that it moved her to tears.[19] Some of Fuentes's surviving stage designs for *Tito* may have been used in this production (Plate 9).

Another early nineteenth-century production of *Tito* in which beautifully designed and executed sets played an important role was at La Scala in 1818. We can sense in Alessandro Sanquirico's design for the Capitol, preserved in a series of engravings of stage

CAMPIDOGLIO
Op: La Clemenza di Tito

10   Alessandro Sanquirico, stage design, probably for the production of
Tito at La Scala, Milan, 1818

designs for *Tito* that may have been used in the production at La
Scala, how magnificent sets could enhance the opera's dramatic
effect (Plate 10).

The critical response to performances of *La clemenza di Tito* in
the *Allgemeine musikalische Zeitung* shows that opera-goers in
Germany, Bohemia, and Austria admired *Tito* as a deeply moving
drama when brought to life by singers who could act as well as sing,
and when staged in a manner suited to the spirit of the drama. *Tito*
was popular not only because of the vocal opportunities it gave to
singers, but also because it encouraged lavish and beautiful costumes and sets, and, above all, because it demanded from its
singers, and often received, skillful and committed acting. In
focussing their attention on problems of interpretation rather than
on the opera itself, critics showed confidence in the dramatic
integrity of the opera and in the opera's ability to work in the
theater.

Tito in London

Throughout much of the eighteenth century London was a center of
the composition and performance of *opera seria*, and it continued
to be in the early nineteenth century. We can get some idea of the
attitudes of the sophisticated and enthusiastic supporters of *opera
seria* who made up part of the London audience from the memoirs
of one of these opera-lovers, Richard, second Earl of Mount
Edgcumbe (1764–1839). A chapter in which he deplored the new
styles of opera coming into London around 1820 (he had Rossini in
mind) is particularly revealing of his views on opera seria. It helps
us understand why *La clemenza di Tito* was the first Mozart opera
performed in London and why it was performed so often there
during the early nineteenth century. Mount Edgcumbe complained
of the decline of both recitative and arias, and of the increasing use
of ensembles:

The dialogue, which used to be carried on in recitative, and which in
Metastasio's operas is often so beautiful and interesting, is now cut up (and
rendered unintelligible if it were worth listening to) into *pezzi concertati*,
or long singing conversations, which present a tedious succession of
unconnected, ever-changing motivos . . . Single songs are almost exploded
[that is, have almost disappeared], for which one good reason may be
given, that there are few singers capable of singing them. Even a prima
donna, who would formerly have complained at having less than three or
four airs allotted to her, is now satisfied with one trifling cavatina for a
whole opera.[20]

Mount Edgcumbe evidently regretted the disappearance of the
male sopranos and contraltos, and their replacement with tenors
and basses:

Sopranos have long ceased to exist, but tenors for a long while filled their
place. Now even these have become so scarce, that Italy can produce no
more than two or three very good ones. The generality of voices are basses,
which for want of better are thrust up into the first characters, even in
serious operas where they used only to occupy the last place, to the
manifest injury of melody, and total subversion of harmony, in which
the lowest part is their peculiar province.[21]

Mount Edgcumbe continued at some length, complaining of the
incorporation into serious opera of finales "such as formerly were
never used but at the end of the acts of comic operas, to which alone
they are appropriate." Apart from his distaste for such finales,
"which to my ears are scarcely music, but mere noise," he found
the new style of opera antithetical to the tradition of great singing:

It is evident that in such compositions each individual singer has little room for displaying either a fine voice or good singing, and that power of lungs is more essential than either. Very good singers therefore are scarcely necessary, and it must be confessed that though there are now none so good, neither are there many so bad as I remember in the inferior characters. In these levelling days, equalization has extended itself to the stage and musical profession; and a kind of mediocrity of talent prevails.[22]

In some respects Mozart's *La clemenza di Tito* represented the changes in serious opera of which Mount Edgcumbe complained: he could not have been too happy with its many ensembles and its finales. Yet in other ways *Tito* represented the old traditions and values to which Mount Edgcumbe felt allegiance (old, that is, when he was writing his memoirs in the 1820s). *Tito* kept much of the Metastasian recitative that Mount Edgcumbe found "so beautiful and interesting"; it emphasised the high voices, with four soprano roles and only one bass; with its good number of elaborate arias, it maintained the traditional emphasis on the principal soloists and their virtuosity. These qualities would have made *La clemenza di Tito* attractive to Mount Edgcumbe and to other London opera-lovers who shared his operatic tastes.

One opera-lover who did evidently share Mount Edgcumbe's tastes was W. T. Parke, who witnessed the first performance of *Tito* in London, on 27 March 1806. He wrote of it in his memoirs:

the principal production of the season was Mozart's grand serious opera, 'La Clemenza di Tito,' performed for the first time in England on the 27th of March, for Billington's benefit. In this charming opera Billington, who was ably supported by Braham, made a display of talent rarely witnessed; and the music stamps the composer of it as the greatest musical genius of the age. Mrs. Billington, with whom I had lived on terms of friendly intimacy for several years, sent me a ticket, and requested I would witness the first performance of 'La Clemenza di Tito,' which I did. I was highly gratified with the refined science, elegant taste, and natural simplicity displayed in this fine production. 'La Clemenza di Tito' was the first of Mozart's operas performed in this country.[23]

Parke made no reference to scenery or costume, to specific arias, to ensembles or choruses, or to the first-act finale that so many later critics would focus on as the opera's best number. Instead he remembered the *prima donna* and the *primo uomo*: the soprano Elizabeth Billington (Vitellia) and the tenor John Braham (Sesto, with the role transposed down an octave). This attention to the soloists is typical of the memoirs of both Mount Edgcumbe and Parke. It is typical too of reviews of performances of *Tito* in the

London newspapers, as in this review of the performance attended by Parke:

The Benefit of Billington, the Goddess of Song, was last night as numerously attended as on most former occasions, proving at once her great popularity. The attraction was the Grand Serious Opera of 'La Clemenza di Tito,' composed by Mozart. Braham was loudly encored in one of his Songs in the First Act [presumably "Parto, ma tu, ben mio"]; and Billington was as warmly applauded as ever. All the People of Fashion in town were present.[24]

Whenever it was revived in London during the next two decades *Tito* served the purpose it served in 1806: as a vehicle for the greatest singers in London at the time. Thus, when Angelica Catalani was in London in 1812 and 1813, she sang Vitellia, although she had to be persuaded to take the role, according to Mount Edgcumbe,

for she detested Mozart's music, which keeps the singer too much under the control of the orchestra, and too strictly confined to time, which she is apt to violate. Yet she first introduced to our stage his Nozze di Figaro, in which she acted the part of Susanna admirably.[25]

In general opera-goers in London seem to have demanded from performers of *La clemenza di Tito* less in the way of acting than did opera-goers in Germany; but that does not mean that fine acting was not appreciated and praised, as it was in 1816, when the great French *prima donna* Joséphine Fodor (who also sang Fiordiligi, Zerlina, and the Countess), took the role of Vitellia. Fodor was warmly welcomed, as was Braham, who returned to the role of Sesto after several years absence:

He [Braham] resumes his station at this Theatre with his vocal powers in their fullest vigour, with an accumulation of that experience which is one of the best sources of good taste, and with an augmentation of his ability as an actor, that immediately struck the whole audience with surprise ... Mad. Fodor took the part of Vitellia, and sustained it with an energy and justness of acting that gained the warmest tokens of approbation.[26]

The decline of *Tito*, 1820–1850

A performance of *Tito* in Prague in 1845, over fifty years after it was first performed there, was sparsely attended. A review in the *Allgemeine musikalische Zeitung* called Mozart's opera "noble," but made clear that tastes had moved away from *Tito*:

For the benefit of Mme. Podhorsky a newly prepared performance of Mozart's noble *Titus* was presented, which nevertheless filled the house only partially (an unheard-of occurrence with Mozart's works), although the cast (with the exception of a couple of the minor roles) was a suitable one within the limits of our company. It is undeniable that *Titus*, more than all of Mozart's other works, carries on it the impression of the time in which it was created. Just as the poet followed the form of Italian–French tragedy, and worked out in the decorative Rococo manner of his time great dramatic situations that needed a Shakespeare if they were to be suitably treated, so too the musician remained faithful to the old operatic form, and his genius broke through only in a few isolated moments, for example, in the masterly finale of the first act, which alone outweighs a whole modern opera. Most of the other numbers are only a test for singers, and we acknowledge with pleasure that ours for the most part passed the test.[27]

The criticism of the libretto implied in the sneering phrase "ge-schnörkelten Rococomanier," the admiring reference to Shake-speare, the almost excessive praise of the first-act finale, the dismissal of most of *La clemenza di Tito* to the realm of "Prüfstein der Sänger": all of these views indicate an attitude toward *Tito* very different from that of the early nineteenth century; and they represent a rejection of the eighteenth-century values that created *Tito*. While earlier reviewers had expressed their respect for the dramatic potential of *Tito* through their careful evaluations of singers' acting, this reviewer showed no interest in the way *Tito* was acted in 1845. In avoiding the subject the reviewer implied that the opera was inherently undramatic; this is also implied by the dismissal of most of the opera's arias as "only a test for singers."

As such views became more and more prevalent, *Tito* receded from the repertory in central Europe. As critics and scholars who discussed the opera had fewer and fewer opportunities to see the opera performed on stage, they based their judgments of the opera increasingly on inspection of scores and librettos, and they depended increasingly on the judgments of previous critics and scholars. Thus a critical tradition hostile to *Tito* developed and began to dominate opinion about the opera. With this tradition firmly entrenched, the chances of a successful revival of *Tito* in the theater were further diminished.

In England too *Tito* lost favor with the public, but for reasons somewhat different from those in Germany. One of many ways in which operatic life in London reflected Italian operatic life was in the rapid absorption of new fashions in serious opera. First Rossini, then Donizetti and Bellini caught the attention of the London public in the 1820s and 1830s; few if any serious operas written before 1810 survived in the repertory. *Tito* had to compete not only with these brilliant newcomers, but also with *Don Giovanni* and *Figaro*, which entered the repertory in London only after 1815, and soon came to represent for London audiences all that was most attractive in Mozart's work. Mount Edgcumbe, remembering with regret the transformation of the London operatic repertory that took place around 1820, mentioned *Tito* as one of the victims of the transformation:

So entirely did Rossini engross the stage, that the operas of no other master were ever to be heard, with the exception of those of Mozart, and of his, only Don Giovanni and Le Nozze di Figaro were often repeated. La Clemenza di Tito was occasionally revived, but met with less success.[28]

The review of the performance of *La clemenza di Tito* in Prague in 1845 implied criticism of the opera by calling it "a test for singers." English audiences, with their love for great singing in the Italian tradition of *opera seria*, would have found nothing objectionable in "a test for singers": they expected every good *opera seria* to be such a test. But after 1820 they did not want *Tito* to serve this purpose any longer: they preferred Rossini's *Otello*, Bellini's *Norma* or Donizetti's *Lucia di Lammermoor*.

"*La clemenza di Tito* is considered, from an esthetic point of view, and as a beautiful work of art, Mozart's most perfect work." Thus Franz Xaver Niemetschek, Mozart's first biographer, began his evaluation of *Tito* in 1798.[1] Obvious in his comment is the admiration for Mozart's last opera that inspired hundreds of performances of it during the half-century that followed. Yet there is also in Niemetschek's praise a note of reservation, of caution. Why did he qualify his statement with that odd phrase "in ästhetischer Hinsicht als schönes Kunstwerk?" Was he perhaps implying that *Tito* could be considered "die vollendeteste Arbeit Mozarts" only if certain aspects of the opera were overlooked?

Niemetschek's discussion of *Tito* has a defensive tone about it. After stating that Mozart wrote the opera in only eighteen days (a claim that he was apparently the first to make in print, and one repeated as fact by many critics during the century that followed), he went on to acknowledge what he apparently considered weaknesses of the opera and to point out strengths that balance these weaknesses. The orchestral parts are "modest"; yet they convey "the simplicity, the calm nobility" of the opera. Two of the principal roles were written for Italian virtuosi; thus Mozart was forced to write arias in which they could display their virtuosity. "But what arias!" wrote Niemetschek. "How far they surpass the normal run of bravura arias!" He praised the opera's other pieces as revealing "everywhere the great spirit from which they flowed"; but he singled out three particular numbers as especially fine: the finale of Act I, the rondò "Non più di fiori," and the final chorus of Act II.

The defensiveness, the praise mixed with blame, the claim that the opera was completed in eighteen days, the objection to the pernicious influence of Italian singers, the suspicion of bravura arias, the elevation of particular numbers to the status of masterpieces above the level of the rest of the opera, the special praise for "Non più di fiori" and the first-act finale: all these features of Niemetschek's evaluation appeared again and again in later discussions of *Tito*. They formed part of a tradition of critical response to *Tito*, a tradition that will be referred to here as the "Romantic critical tradition" both because it thrived in the nineteenth century and because it represents certain features of German Romanticism. This Romantic critical tradition dominated opinion of the opera from the middle of the nineteenth century until about 1970 and helped keep *Tito* out of most of the world's opera houses during that period.

The values that informed the Romantic critical tradition are equally evident in such manifestos of Romantic musico-dramatic esthetics as Richard Wagner's *Oper und Drama*. Wagner's antipathies toward the French classical theater that so markedly influenced Metastasio's librettos, toward the aria as a musical and dramatic entity, and toward simple recitative, all well documented in *Oper und Drama*, are attitudes he shared with writers who found much to criticize in *Tito*. Wagner said little about *Tito* itself. He called it, in passing, "stiff and dry" (*steif und trocken*)[2] and, in a famous passage in *Oper und Drama*, he praised Mozart for not writing the same kind of music for *Tito* that he had written for *Don Giovanni*:

Oh how truly dear and most praiseworthy is Mozart for me, that it was *not* possible for him to invent music for *Tito* like that of *Don Giovanni*, for *Così fan tutte* like that of *Figaro*! How disgracefully it would have desecrated music![3]

But if Wagner had expressed himself more fully on the subject of *Tito*, his discussion would have probably covered much the same ground as those of other critics who considered the opera after about 1840, and would have criticized it just as harshly.

This chapter examines some of the themes common to writers in the Romantic critical tradition, with special attention to two of the most important mid-nineteenth-century writers on Mozart: the Russian music critic Alexander Dmitryevich Ulibishev (or Oulibicheff) and the German classicist and Mozart scholar Otto Jahn. Ulibishev, son of the Russian ambassador at Dresden, grew up and received his musical education there; in this center of nineteenth-century German musical culture he had the opportunity to hear many operas, including *Tito*. In his three-volume biography of Mozart (Moscow, 1843) Ulibishev devoted to *Tito* what was then the most detailed evaluation of the opera.[4] It is also a clear exposition of the Romantic critical tradition. Jahn, who published the first edition of his great biography of Mozart between 1856 and 1859,[5] wrote his work during the same decade in which Wagner wrote *Oper und Drama* (1850–51), the libretto for the *Ring* (1852), and the scores of *Das Rheingold* (1854), *Die Walküre* (1856) and *Tristan und Isolde* (1859). Not surprisingly we can see in Jahn's views on *La clemenza di Tito* many of the attitudes behind *Oper und Drama* and behind Wagner's music dramas. And just as *Oper und Drama* exercised profound influence over attitudes toward opera for more than a century after its publication, so Jahn's views on *La clemenza di Tito* resonated in critical writing about that opera during the same period.

Looking at what some twentieth-century Mozart scholars have said about *Tito*, we can see the pervasiveness with which the Romantic critical tradition has influenced thinking about the opera, and to some extent continues to do so. Edward Dent, who published the first edition of his *Mozart's operas* in 1913, was still very much within the tradition.[6] Alfred Einstein, who published *Mozart: his character, his work* in 1945, attempted at times to break away from the tradition, but was still very much influenced by it.[7] So was Anna Amalie Abert, whose criticism of *Tito* in the *New Oxford history of music* (1973) stands in stark contrast to the revival of interest in and appreciation for *Tito* among scholars, singers and opera-lovers that was taking place around the same time. Abert's critique reads in hindsight like the last stand of an obsolete ideology. Repudiation of the Romantic critical tradition was a necessary part of the process of re-evaluation of *Tito* and its reinstatement in the repertory.

A product of illness, haste, and reluctance

Most writers in the Romantic critical tradition included in their discussions of *La clemenza di Tito* some reference to the disadvantages under which Mozart worked when writing the opera. Most, like Jahn, listed these disadvantages as a way of explaining why the opera is weak. A few, like Ulibishev, who sought to emphasize the opera's beauties, mentioned the disadvantages as a way of increasing their readers' appreciation for those beauties.

After criticizing the libretto at great length, Jahn went on to summarize the other difficulties that Mozart had to bear. First, he had to write for a specific occasion and as the result of a commission.

Jahn's implication, typically Romantic, is that a great work of art must come from within; it must result from inspiration, not from a commission. Second, Mozart had to write for Italian virtuosi who "would demand to be shown at their best." The implication is that great operas can be written only when the composer has singers who are willing to submit to his genius. (Jahn fails to consider here Mozart's practice, of which there is ample evidence in his letters, of constantly seeking to show his singers at their best; singers had no need to demand such treatment from him.) Third, Mozart had to compose the opera quickly and during an illness. Jahn evidently assumed that for an opera to be a great work of art, it had to be the product not only of inspiration but of long and painstaking labor, as were those of his contemporary Wagner. He concluded: "it will scarcely be expected that an unqualified success should follow such a combination of untoward circumstances."

Edward Dent saw Mozart faced with many of the same difficulties. "The opera was finished in eighteen days ... by a man in broken health, exhausted by overwork, and forced to write in haste against his will." This melodramatic view of Mozart's mental state and the speed with which he worked, with all the implications that it entails for the quality of the opera he produced, is very much in the Romantic critical tradition.

Einstein was more realistic. Although he agreed that *Tito* was a product of haste, he must have found suspect Niemetschek's claim, repeated by so many nineteenth-century writers, that Mozart wrote the opera in eighteen days; he did not repeat it. As for fatigue and illness, Einstein pointed out that *Tito* could not have been the product of a fatigue or illness that limited Mozart's creative energy; or how could we explain *Die Zauberflöte* and the completed portions of the *Requiem*?

Einstein said nothing about Mozart's composing *Tito* against his will; rather he implied the opposite by suggesting that Mozart approved of Mazzolà's revision of Metastasio's libretto, citing Mozart's entry of *Tito* in his work-list, where the composer described his libretto as having been *ridotta a vera opera* ("reduced to true opera") by Mazzolà.

The genre, the libretto and the revision

Typical of the Romantic critical tradition is the tendency to dismiss *opera seria* as a genre that was old-fashioned at the time Mozart wrote *La clemenza di Tito*. Jahn referred to the genre as "the old *opera seria*," the features of which bound Mozart "to forms and dogmas which were virtually obsolete," and which "Mozart had abandoned long ago." He did not mention that even if Mozart had wanted to write *opera seria* in Vienna during the 1780s he could not have done so owing to Joseph II's lack of interest in the genre. Einstein, writing almost a century later, expressed much the same view: "The *opera seria* in 1790 was already an artifact, a fossil relic of earlier cultural strata."

Ulibishev's criticism of Metastasio's libretto is an example of the tendency of the Romantic critical tradition to criticize *opera seria* for what it lacked rather than to appreciate it for what it was:

Metastasio's poem, in its original form, was poorly conceived and poorly suited to the framework and the proportions of modern opera, since it offers, in course of a languid plot stretched out over three acts, nothing more than a succession of arias and recitatives.

Ulibishev was dissatisfied with the content of the libretto as well as its structure. After pointing out the relationship between Metastasio's *La clemenza di Tito* and Corneille's *Cinna, ou la clémence d'Auguste* ("The Italian poem lacks only the beauties of the French tragedy; with these the resemblance would be complete."), he argued that history had never been a good source for operatic plots. His view may reflect the comparative rarity of historical plots in German Romantic opera.

Jahn began his discussion of *Tito* by criticizing Metastasio's libretto even more thoroughly and harshly than Ulibishev. He found no dramatic interest in either the plot or the characters. Tito's clemency he criticized as "abstract goodness" that is undramatic because it is predictable. Here Jahn seems to have forgotten the painful dilemmas that Tito has to face before deciding to pardon Sesto; he seems to have forgotten too that during several scenes near the end of the opera all the characters except Tito himself believe that he has signed Sesto's death sentence. Jahn criticized Publio, Annio, and Servilia as "mere props in the plot, characters without any individuality." He criticized Sesto as "a purely passive instrument, wavering between love and remorse, without force or decision." Demonstrating a moralistic side of the Romantic critical tradition, Jahn expressed revulsion for Vitellia's "bare-faced ambition, to which she is ready to sacrifice every sentiment and every duty"; but Jahn was not satisfied even by Vitellia's repentence: "her remorse comes too late to appear anything but a dissonance leading to the inevitable conclusion."

Jahn was equally unimpressed by Metastasio's "dainty style," which, he argued, "was specially suited for court poetry and its corresponding musical expression." Here again we can sense something moralistic in Jahn's response, a kind of righteous indignation. Metastasio's style encouraged a taste "for mere amusement of the trifling kind that was looked for at the opera at that time, giving an unseemly effeminacy of tone to the *opera seria*, and running an equal risk of degenerating into mere trifling or empty pomp and show."

Neither Dent nor Einstein found anything to praise in Metastasio's original libretto. Dent called it "a pompous and frigid drama of Roman history." Einstein, echoing Ulibishev, dismissed it as "nothing but a chain of exit arias, joined together by long recitatives; there is no provision even for the smallest duet." Although he qualified this description by acknowledging that Metastasio wrote his libretto "in accordance with the practice of the *opera seria* in 1734," he followed Ulibishev in avoiding any suggestion that the libretto should be evaluated within the framework of the conventions that produced it. Einstein went on to criticize Metastasio's characters as "puppets"; his discussion seems to reflect his knowledge of Jahn's opinions more than a thoughtful and sympathetic reading of the libretto.

Most writers in the Romantic critical tradition had praise for at least some aspects of Mazzolà's revision. Ulibishev found that Mazzolà greatly improved the libretto by reducing Metastasio's dialogue and incorporating ensembles. Einstein too was pleased with the revision, though he could not resist a condescending comment as well: "What Mazzolà did with this libretto is evidence not of lack of respect but of courage and ingenuity ... Naturally Mazzolà could not make a masterpiece out of Metastasio's court libretto ... But he made the libretto a hundred times more effective." Jahn and Dent were less enthusiastic. Jahn, while praising Mozart's setting of Mazzolà's ensemble-texts, claimed that Mazzolà's revision "did not affect the character of the opera in any important degree." Dent too praised Mozart's ensembles, but faulted Mazzolà for having created "a rather shapeless opera."

Ulibishev credited Mozart with instigating and directing the revisions, without however citing any evidence: "Mozart saw the necessity of recasting the libretto before being able to set it to music, which Mazzolà accomplished according to the ideas and under the direction of the composer." Behind this claim are typically Romantic notions of creativity: that a single mind must be behind a work of art; that a single musician must be responsible for bringing an opera to dramatic life. Since writers in the Romantic critical tradition almost universally agreed that the first-act finale was the greatest single movement in *La clemenza di Tito*, it is not surprising that these same writers tended to assign a particularly important role to Mozart in the development of this finale. Ulibishev claimed, again without evidence, that Mozart "supervised the preparation of the poetry" of the finale. Although Dent did not go that far, he did credit Mozart with the entrance of the off-stage chorus during the finale, singing "horribly dramatic cries of 'Ah!' "[8]

A soprano hero and vocal virtuosity

In the eyes of both Ulibishev and Jahn, the fact that Mozart wrote two male roles, Sesto and Annio, for sopranos seriously weakened *Tito*. Their views on this issue reflect the nineteenth century's feelings of revulsion towards the *musico* and its distaste for the practice, common in early nineteenth-century Italy, of having women sing the roles of young male heroes. Most writers in the Romantic critical tradition felt that a soprano hero was unseemly, unnatural and undramatic, whether that soprano was a man or a woman. Ulibishev and Jahn mistakenly believed that the role of Sesto was created by a female singer. But even if they had known that the *musico* Domenico Bedini created the role of Sesto, their esthetic and moral indignation would have been just as strongly expressed. Ulibishev put it this way: "To heroes and tragic lovers, conspirators, and regicides whose vocal part is written in the soprano or contralto clef, the rules of musical criticism cannot seriously be applied in matters of dramatic truth." Jahn was even more vehement:

The fact that the parts of the lovers, Sextus and Annius, were soprano, was an objectionable relic of the old opera seria, and that Sextus should have been played by a female and not a male soprano was a progress indeed for humanity, but not for the drama. True characterization is impossible when a woman in man's clothes plays the lover, and the case is not improved by the weak, womanish character of Sextus. His passion for Vitellia becomes a thing contrary to nature, and the deeper the dramatic conception of the part the more repulsively does this appear. Of necessity, therefore, vocal execution comes to the foreground.

"Vocal execution comes to the foreground": this was anathema to the Romantic critic. From Niemetschek to the recent past, writers in the Romantic critical tradition have deplored the influence on *Tito* of the Italian virtuosi for whom it was written; they doubtless assumed that Mozart would have preferred to write less floridly for serious, German singers, and that *Tito* would have been better if he had done so. These critics seem to have rarely considered what Mozart knew well: that vocal virtuosity can itself be a source of intense drama on the operatic stage.

The division of the opera into strong and weak parts

The journalist and critic Friedrich Rochlitz, writing of *La clemenza di Tito* in the *Allgemeine musikalische Zeitung* in 1798–99, made the influential suggestion that Mozart, pressed for time, chose to concentrate his efforts on a few numbers. Assigning the simple recitative to an assistant and setting some of the less important numbers in a simple style, "light and suited to the tastes of the public," Mozart devoted most of his energy and creativity to "the principal numbers."[9] Ulibishev, without acknowledging his source, repeated Rochlitz's account almost verbatim. He developed it further, arguing that critics' views of *Tito* differed "according to whether the critics have viewed the work as a whole or in its details. As a whole, it is without doubt the least perfect of the composer's seven classic operas." Ulibishev then went on to discuss the opera's defects at some length, and continued: "After having sided with the opera's critics, let us now assure ourselves, to be fair, that none of Mozart's operas except *Idomeneo* and *Don Giovanni* contains dramatic beauties of such an exalted order as this same *La clemenza di Tito*."

This division of the opera, for the purposes of critical appraisal, into a weak whole with some beautiful parts, influenced much thought about *Tito*, including that of Dent, who argued that the weaker parts of the opera, in which Mozart "purposely adopted a plain and easy style with obvious melodies of old-fashioned cut, the simplest harmonies, and the thinnest orchestration," would appeal to coronation audiences.

One of the most serious charges that critics in the Romantic tradition aimed at *Tito* is that the tone of Mozart's music is often unsuited to the seriousness of the drama. Ulibishev devoted much attention to this charge. Not only did Mozart "weaken many of the drama's truly tragic scenes," he said, "but he went so far as to make himself pleasant and sentimental where he should have been pathetic and terrible, to the extent of obvious absurdity." To back up this accusation Ulibishev cited Sesto's rondò "Deh per questo istante solo," describing the dramatic situation and then turning to the aria itself:

Sesto is led before Tito, his friend, his benefactor and now his judge, whom he tried to assassinate. The guilty one expresses the horror of remorse that tortures him and asks, as a last favor, for a prompt punishment. Certainly, nothing could be less ambiguous than a situation like this one. Now, if Sesto, whose sister Caesar wants to marry, Sesto, overwhelmed with imperial favor, had to thank his master "di tante grazie," would he not have chosen a melody other than "Tanto affanno soffre un core nè si more di dolor?" But Mozart – yes, Mozart–: what was he dreaming of when he chose it? He was dreaming, it seems, of Signora Perini, a good singer, perhaps, probably a bad actress, and in any case a woman, to whom the role of Sesto had been entrusted.

Ulibishev referred here to the principal melody of the rondò's fast section, a melody quoted and discussed in chapter 5 (see Ex. 39). The only explanation that Ulibishev could propose for this senti-mental tune was that Mozart was writing for a woman. If he had known that this melody was written not for a woman but a male soprano (Carolina Perini sang the role of Annio, not Sesto), Ulibishev's disapproval would not have been mollified.

Jahn's opinion of "Deh per questo istante solo" was mixed. He praised the opening slow section as "fervent and true, and the softness characterising it belongs to the character and the situ-ation." But he agreed with Ulibishev (without referring to him) about the theme of the fast section: "the second movement expresses a certain amount of passion in some parts, but is as a whole wanting in energy, and its chief motif, even for a female Sextus, is too soft and tender."

As long as writers in the Romantic critical tradition continued to isolate a few numbers in *Tito* and point to them as individual masterpieces, one of the numbers that consistently appeared on their lists was Vitellia's rondò "Non più di fiori." Already Nie-metschek could think of no aria "so lovely, so full of sweet melancholy, so rich in musical beauties, as the perfect rondo in F with obbligato basset horn, 'Non più di fiori,' in the second act." Few commentators in the Romantic critical tradition have dared to differ from this judgement.

For Ulibishev "Non più di fiori" was "the most beautiful aria in the opera and one of the most beautiful that Mozart ever wrote." Ulibishev, giving himself over to Romantic sentimentality, saw a parallel between the second stanza of the aria-text

Stretta fra barbare
Aspre ritorte
Veggo la morte
Ver me avanzar.

Bound in sharp, cruel chains, I see death advancing towards me.

and Mozart's own approaching death: "Mozart likewise saw the dark figure cutting him off from the season of flowers, which would never bloom again, except on his tomb." He went on to praise the aria in extravagant terms:

There are few vocal pieces known to us in which so many noble musical ideas have been brought together as in this aria, and few whose character is more difficult to define ... The aria is so wonderfully beautiful, the lament is so delightfully shaped by the free play of the musician's imagination, the inexpressible meaning of the motives is so superior to that of the words, the melodies of the *obbligato* instrument repeat with such sweet echoes the vocal phrases, anticipating and commenting on thoughts with so much charm, everything, in short, rises to such a height of perfection ...

But Ulibishev could not resist the temptation to criticize even this aria: "On the other hand, it is true that this enchanting, divine aria expresses rather badly, or rather it does not express at all Vitellia's character, which is that of a madwoman and a monster."

Jahn praised "Non più di fiori" as enthusiastically as Ulibishev, and, like Ulibishev, he criticized it as well. He agreed that Vitellia's character as portrayed here was inconsistent with her character as developed earlier in the opera. This inconsistency, suggested Jahn, with implied disapproval, gave "Non più di fiori" the quality of a concert aria. "Vitellia's second air ... is the gem of the opera, and incontestably one of the most beautiful songs ever written." Yet the aria seems "to be detached from the framework of the opera, and to belong rather to the province of concert music." Jahn comes close to forgiving Mozart for the concert-aria-like quality of "Non più di fiori":

Every element of the song is blended into such perfect unity, such charm of melody, such beauty of musical form; the sharp contrasts of the different motifs are so admirably expressive of the general character of which they form the details, and the whole work is so permeated by the breath of poetic genius, that our satisfaction in contemplating a perfect work of art leads us to forget how it stands forth as something foreign to the context.

Dent agreed, referring to "Parto, ma tu, ben mio" as well as "Non più di fiori": "In the opera both arias stand out as concert-pieces."

"Altogether worthy of Mozart": The first-act finale

The Romantic critics agreed that Mozart exercised his skills as a dramatic composer most effectively in ensembles, which are, in Ulibishev's words, "so favorable to the deployment of theatrical music's greatest effects." No wonder that Ulibishev and other nineteenth-century critics of *La clemenza di Tito* directed much of their attention to the work's ensembles, in which "Mozart allows his dramatic genius more freedom" than in the arias, according to Dent. And no wonder that they directed much of their praise to the most elaborate of these ensembles, the finale of Act I. Niemetschek called it "certainly Mozart's finest work: expression, character, and feeling vie with one another to produce the greatest effect"; Ulibishev called it "the crown of the entire work." Jahn singled out the finale as the "one movement . . . altogether worthy of Mozart"; and more than fifty years later Dent called it "the finest movement of all." The tendency for writers in the Romantic critical tradition to credit Mozart rather than Mazzolà with the conception of this finale is an indication of the depth of admiration that these critics felt for the finale; for how could such a musical and dramatic tour de force have been conceived except by a single genius? And what genius contributed to *Tito* but Mozart?

Ulibishev's long and detailed discussion of the finale helps us understand how this movement affected nineteenth-century critics. Imagining the scene with Romantic sensibility, Ulibishev assumed that it took place at night, though there is nothing in Mozart's opera to suggest that this is the case. Ulibishev's discussion deserves to be quoted at some length.

A nocturnal scene, in the middle of the Forum, soon to be illuminated by the flames of the burning Capitol; Sextus, opening the finale with a monologue in which he tries to steel himself to the idea of parricide; the other characters arriving in succession, and each with a reason: some tortured with remorse, some full of horror and dismay, the murderer who leaves and returns, a new Orestes with the furies at his footsteps, the revolt rumbling everywhere, and the Roman people, the chorus, who cry out in despair, who play the principal part in this drama, both epic and tragic: let us agree that nothing could be more beautiful; nothing could be more musical.

Mozart the composer did not fall below Mozart the arranger of the libretto. His poetic ideas aroused his musical ones, they stirred him up, they inspired him . . . never has a greater or more grandiose conception been offered for the admiration of men . . .

The Allegro of the Quintet, in spite of its extraordinary scenic effect and the tumultuous movement that dominates it, is constructed thematically. The unity of the composition resides in a vocal phrase restated in different keys, both major and minor, which the characters take up one after another, as each arrives. Between these phrases, nobly pathetic and yet always melodious, fall the harrowing cries of the chorus behind the scenes. You hear them as the cries of agony of a people under whose feet a gigantic grave has opened up. The great mass of the orchestra breaks with a thundering crash on these cries of distress, first heard at long intervals, and one outburst at a time: "Ah!" These explosions, taking place on various harmonies of the diminished seventh, lead each time to a different key. Gradually the great voice of the people approaches; the cries of the chorus become more frequent and come in groups of two: "Ah! Ah!"

Such is the musical organization of this Allegro. As for its effect, that is above any description. One must hear this music, performed as it should be, by artists who are both good actors and good singers, supported by a large and excellent chorus, and with a proper staging.

Mozart let himself be moved sometimes by a wonderful spirit of paradox. What musician would have thought of ending this finale with an Andante, when the dramatic situation has not apparently changed? Who would not have predicted that the overwhelming effect of the Allegro would thereby be dissipated and that the thousands of hands raised in readiness to applaud would finally fall into the laps of the audience? Mozart did not care in the least: he stopped right in the middle of the Allegro, in order to write two or three lines of the simplest recitative, and he began his Andante very tranquilly. He knew well what he was doing. His idea was bold, but not paradoxical. We were saying that the situation did not seem to have changed. Physically no; but psychologically yes, a great deal. When, at the beginning of the finale, Sextus leaves to attack his victim, the conspiracy is already underway, the Capitol is on fire, the people who do not know the cause or the motive of what they see run through the city, crying out in terror; but when Sextus returns, thinking that he has committed his crime, the news of the attempted assassination of Titus must have already spread through Rome with the speed of lightning. The people have learned all, and because the first effect of a great disaster is to strike dumb the imagination, the music must express an intense horror, pale, immobile features, a kind of mental paralysis. This is not my reasoning, but Mozart's. The Andante is its inescapable consequence, and also its brilliant justification. It is something even more sublime than the Allegro.

Here, the disposition of vocal parts is altogether different. The chorus, having arrived on the stage, no longer interrupts with exclamations, but proceeds with regular, complete phrases: "Oh nero tradimento! Oh giorno di dolor!" and enters into dialogue with the solo characters, who form another chorus. A third group, composed of flutes, oboes, clarinets, bassoons, horns, trumpets, and timpani, strike up a lugubrious martial rhythm. One thinks one is hearing a funeral bell toll for public happiness, dead along with Titus. Starting with the measure in which Vitellia and Servilia, ascending the scale from the tonic, arrive at a C flat ("Oh – gior – no – di – do – lor") the dialogue of the double chorus is composed with an art whose secret our hero inherited from no one and bequeathed to no one. Three times the expected cadence falls on dissonant, grating chords, so that this passage, a passage unique and forever to be celebrated, does not arrive at its conclusion until the twenty-second measure. The timpani rumble quietly at the final cadence; the clamor of this disastrous night disappears gradually in its shadows. Tragic majesty, terror, and pity have never been taken further on the musical stage.

The enthusiasm of Ulibishev's discussion suggests not only why the Romantic critical tradition valued this finale so highly, but also why it found much of the rest of the opera weak in comparison. Writers in this tradition looked for the "tragic majesty, terror, and pity" of the finale and could not find it elsewhere in the opera. Jahn concluded his description of the finale with a note of regret: "Here we may perceive to what height opera seria was capable of rising by a liberal development of its original contents; but unfortunately this movement is the only one of its kind in *Titus*." Other critics must have felt this same regret. With its powerful theatricality, its strong appeal to the Romantic imagination, Mozart's first-act finale may well have contributed to the Romantics' lack of appreciation for and misunderstanding of *La clemenza di Tito* as a whole.

The survival of the Romantic critical tradition: Kerman and A. A. Abert

The Romantic critical tradition survives to the present, and contributes to continued misunderstanding of *La clemenza di Tito*. Joseph Kerman's discussion of *opera seria* in *Opera as drama* (1956, revised 1988) represents a kind of codification of the Romantic critical tradition, persuasively articulating some of its most characteristic attitudes.[10] Some recent discussions of *La clemenza di Tito* continue to base their evaluations on the Romantic critical tradition, among them Anna Amalie Abert's comments in *The new Oxford history of music* (1973).

One of the most important ideas behind Kerman's view of opera is that of the composer as dramatist ("the dramatist is the composer.") Kerman puts the composer at the top of the operatic enterprise, above librettist, singers, and stage director. The idea of composer as supreme dramatist (an idea at the center of Wagner's *Oper und Drama*, and of which Wagner himself is an obvious personification) carries with it many implications for eighteenth-century opera. One of the victims of such a view is the eighteenth-century opera composer, who viewed himself not as supreme dramatist but as a collaborator with poet and singers, all of whom were expected to contribute as much to the opera's dramatic effect as the composer. The poet and singers, for example, were primarily responsible for the success of the simple recitative, in which the drama is conveyed primarily in words and action rather than in music, and over which the composer could exert little influence. A genre like *opera seria*, in which much of the drama takes place in simple recitative, cannot possibly be dramatic, in Kerman's view, no matter how skillful the composer is. That is one reason why he refers to the history of opera between Monteverdi and Mozart as the "Dark Ages." The only kind of Italian opera in which an eighteenth-century composer could succeed as a musical dramatist was *opera buffa*, because the many ensembles of *opera buffa* allowed the composer to deal, in music, with much of the action and characterization that *opera seria* assigned to simple recitative.

Such a fundamentally flawed genre as *opera seria* could not possibly survive for long; so Kerman follows the Romantic critical tradition in believing that *opera seria* was a dying genre when Mozart wrote *Tito* (for Kerman *opera seria* was "aged and under attack" even when Mozart wrote *Idomeneo*). Also characteristic of the Romantic critical tradition is Kerman's view of singers, whom he sees as a harmful influence on *opera seria*, quoting Dent: "the great and the small [composers] were equally at the mercy of singers." At the same time Kerman gives little attention to what singers contributed (and can today contribute) to *opera seria* in their acting and their singing, singing that often included (and should today include) elaborate and expressive improvisation. The Romantic critical tradition built and continues to build its judgments of *opera seria* on the music as written down: Kerman makes no more effort than did Jahn or Dent to understand *opera seria* as it was performed and applauded in the eighteenth century.

Kerman, like Wagner, mentions *Tito* only in passing; clearly it does not belong in the "significant operatic canon" as he defines it. Nor is it considered a successful opera by those critics who continue to evaluate opera along the lines defined by the Romantic critical tradition and re-enforced by Kerman's study. One such critic is Anna Amalie Abert, daughter of Hermann Abert, the editor of Jahn's biography of Mozart, and an influential heir to the Romantic critical tradition.[11]

Abert's article on the operas of Mozart in *The new Oxford*

history of music is full of assumptions, often implied rather than expressed, typical of the Romantic critical tradition: that *opera seria*, as an expression of the cultural values of the *ancien régime*, had fallen along with the Bastille in 1789; that the conventionality of Metastasio's librettos made them dramatically weak, that arias should avoid vocal virtuosity for its own sake, and that Mozart's ensembles tend to be more dramatic than his arias.

Abert, following Jahn, argues that Mazzolà's revision was a failure since it did not remove "the overall conventionality characteristic of *opera seria*," and since "all of the characters remain pale and schematic." She claims that Mozart wanted nothing to do with *opera seria*: "A decade earlier he had himself liberalized the conventions of the genre in *Idomeneo* and had abandoned them entirely in the masterpieces composed since." (Here Abert follows Jahn again: "*opera seria*, which Mozart had abandoned long ago . . ."; like Jahn, she fails to consider the circumstances that kept Mozart away from *opera seria* during the 1780s.) She concludes that Mozart could not have written *Tito* with any interest or enthusiasm:

That he should accept a commission of this kind while engaged on *Die Zauberflöte* is to be explained solely by dire financial necessities. Still, to the modern student it seems almost macabre to see the composer of Sarastro's creed caught in the toils of dated conventions, whether courtly or operatic or both.

Abert's distaste for vocal virtuosity is an aspect of the Romantic critical tradition that can be traced all the way back to Niemetschek; she calls the arias "Parto, ma tu, ben mio" and "Non più di fiori" beautiful "in spite of the acknowledgement of the virtuoso quality of the singers." Like Niemetschek almost a century and a half before, Abert singles out for special praise Vitellia's rondò. Of Mozart's arias, she writes, " 'Non più di fiori' is the only one we may consider a dramatic as well as a musical masterpiece, to be set alongside the first finale."

Like so many critics before her, Abert praises Mazzolà's incorporation of ensembles; she calls them his "most forward-looking innovation." But she does not value all ensembles equally. Her comment about the trio "Vengo . . . aspettate . . . Sesto! . . ." reveals one of the standards implied in her judgments. She describes it as "more like an expression of the heroine's despair, to which the other two voices supply a background, than a dialogue between three equals." The implication that an ensemble should somehow be "a dialogue between equals" can be traced back to

Jahn, who criticized this trio on exactly the same grounds, arguing that all three trios "fail to elicit dramatic contrasts by giving to each character an equal and characteristic share in the piece. Thus, in the first terzet, Vitellia alone is inspired with lively emotion, Annius and Publius being mere passive spectators." Abert makes explicit what was probably behind many of her judgments (and those of her predecessors in the Romantic critical tradition): a normally unspoken comparison between *Tito* and Mozart's comic operas, *Figaro* and *Don Giovanni* in particular. She praises the duet "Come ti piace imponi" and the trios "Se al volto mai ti senti" and "Quello di Tito è il volto" as numbers in which "the composer turned the first part into a colloquy between sharply differentiated personalities and the second into a musically co-ordinated ensemble." This, according to Abert, represented "a happy compromise between dramatic and musical requirements, even though not comparable with the ensembles in *Figaro* and *Don Giovanni*."

There are few ideas in Abert's discussion of *La clemenza di Tito* that were not already expressed by Ulibishev, Jahn, Dent, or Einstein, just as Kerman's views on *opera seria* in general reflect those of Wagner and Dent. Building on over a century and a half of the Romantic critical tradition, Abert's discussion of *Tito* is an illustration of what happens when the views expressed by Kerman are applied to *Tito*. The noticeable lack of originality in her discussion, her inability to find new meaning in *Tito* is an indication that the Romantic critical tradition, although it survives to the present and continues to influence opinion, has little of interest to contribute to our understanding or appreciation of *La clemenza di Tito*.

8 Performance and critical re-evaluation since 1949

Once an opera leaves the repertory it is hard to bring it back. Operatic criticism tends to guard against the return of works into the repertorial fold; the assumption seems to be that if a work is not performed, there must be some good reason for its absence. Some critics seem to consider it their job to find new ways to legitimize the traditional canon of operatic masterpieces without adding new works to that canon. Part of the problem is that it is difficult to appreciate an opera unless it is performed successfully on stage and on recordings. Yet to perform an opera successfully directors, conductors, and singers first of all need to appreciate it, to take it seriously both as music and as drama. Critical appreciation and successful performance depend on one another. It should come as no surprise that deepening appreciation for *La clemenza di Tito* has coincided with a series of skillful and successful productions of the opera. The best of these productions have shared at least one important thing. They have demonstrated confidence in *Tito*'s intrinsic strength: the ability of the work itself to move modern audiences.

1949–1968: Efforts to improve a defective opera

Many productions of *La clemenza di Tito* before 1970 betrayed a marked lack of confidence, on the part of directors, conductors, and singers, in the opera's merits. Strongly influenced by the Romantic critical tradition, directors tried to improve the opera, both words and music; their efforts implied an attitude of distrust, even disdain toward the opera as Metastasio, Mazzolà, and Mozart wrote it. The almost inevitable result of such "improvements" was that audiences, who came to the opera suspicious of its merits, were confirmed in their suspicions.

The Salzburg Festival production of 1949 presented *La clemenza*

134

di Tito in a version heavily edited by Bernhard Paumgartner and Hans Curjel, who removed most of the simple recitative, omitted several arias, and added several excerpts from *Idomeneo*, including the great quartet. In a curious attempt to return to the shape of Metastasio's original libretto, they recast the opera in three acts, relegating Mozart's first-act finale to the middle of Act II and decking out the opera with orchestral interludes derived from *Idomeneo* and from Mozart's incidental music to the play *Thamos, König in Aegypten*. This patchwork, conducted by Josef Krips, did not succeed in convincing audiences that *La clemenza di Tito* was a viable opera. *Tito* was not presented again at Salzburg for more than a quarter of a century. Unfortunately the effect of the production went far beyond Salzburg: a vocal score of the Paumgartner–Curjel revision was published soon after (Zurich, 1953) and it exercised an insidious influence on many productions of *Tito* during the subsequent two decades.

Another production in which those responsible seem to have lacked confidence in the drama was the performance of *Tito* in English translation at the Berkshire Music Festival in Tanglewood, Massachusetts, in 1952 (Plate 11). Writing of this production, apparently the first staging of *Tito* in the United States, Elizabeth

11   First American staging of *Tito*, Tanglewood, Massachusetts, 4–5 August 1952

Caswell repeated much of the received opinion: that the genre of *opera seria* was old-fashioned at the time when Mozart wrote *Tito*, that "the story exaggerated royalty's virtue and goodness, and was hypocritical and insincere." No wonder, then, that the libretto had to be rewritten for Tanglewood: "Indefatigable Boris Goldovsky [stage director and conductor] and capable Sarah Caldwell [his assistant] revised and translated the text and humanized Titus' character."[1] Exactly what "humanized" means is not clear; but Caswell's remarks did not bode well for a successful revival of *La clemenza di Tito* in the United States. *New York Times* critic Howard Taubman called the production "further proof of what the scholars have long contended – that this is fundamentally a weak piece"[2] and according to Jay Harrison of the New York *Herald Tribune*, "there were moments last night in which "Titus" fell flat on its face."[3] In spite of some favorable reaction to the Tanglewood performances (according to Caswell, Leonard Bernstein said that *Tito* was "very fine, and should be done at the Metropolitan immediately"), the opera was not apparently staged in New York until 1971, and did not reach the Metropolitan Opera until 1984.

When *Tito* was performed in Düsseldorf in 1967 Horst Koegler expressed what seems to have been the standard view at the time: "To encounter *La clemenza di Tito* is so rare that one is grateful for every production, though one knows that it will be a flop dramatically." Having begun his own review thus, how could Koegler blame the directors Georg Reinhardt and Heinrich Wendel for not trying "to mobilize all the remaining energies of the score rather than aim for a costumed *concerto scenico*, resulting in 150 minutes of rarely relieved, beautiful boredom?" And how could he be surprised at the soloists' singing, which he described as "listless, completely unengaged, and depersonalized," and at the "lethargic conducting" of Günther Wich? "One knows it will be a flop dramatically": stage directors, conductor, and singers all seem to have shared Koegler's own view of the work that they were performing; each confirmed the others' opinions.[4]

A production of *La clemenza di Tito* at the Juilliard School in 1971, possibly the first staged production of the opera in New York, likewise seems to have had only the half-hearted support of those behind it and of audiences who saw it. As in Salzburg much of the dialogue was cut, and again arias were added from other sources: "Vado, ma dove?" (K. 583, written by Mozart in 1789 for insertion in Martín y Soler's *Il burbero di buon cuore*) for Servilia in Act I, and "Vorrei spiegarvi, oh Dio" (K. 418, written by Mozart for insertion in Anfossi's *Il curioso indiscreto* in 1783) for Vitellia in Act II, according to a critic from the *New York Times* who saw the performance. From his review, which repeats much of the conventional wisdom about the opera's defects ("The characters exhibit stock emotions with all the human sensibility of a wooden Indian"), we can guess that the critic carried into the theater attitudes shaped by the Romantic critical tradition; and evidently the production did nothing to dispel his prejudices.[5]

A recording of *La clemenza di Tito* released in 1968 carried the same mixed message as these productions: that the opera is full of musical beauties but that it does not and cannot work as drama. Although the producer Erik Smith argued in his notes that " 'Tito' must have its place among the great Mozart operas," he undercut his argument by repeating, and failing to contradict, old judgments: "It is undoubtedly static in its stage-craft, wooden in its characterisation, when one thinks of the life and humanity of Mozart's other masterpieces." Smith called *opera seria* "a dull formal medium" and asked incredulously: "Why would Mozart at this stage of his career *choose* to write in the form of opera seria which was as dead as a door nail by 1791 and had really never been very much alive?"[6]

Not surprisingly the opera that Smith presented on record is indeed as wooden as he claimed, the vitality of the drama having been drained away, above all, by drastic cutting of simple recitative to about half its original length, and by the performance of the remaining recitative with "the measured tread of antique tragedy," as Smith put it. He justified the cuts partly on the grounds that the simple recitatives are not by Mozart, but he had other reasons as well: he cut the whole opening dialogue between Sesto and Vitellia because "*secco* recitative (especially Süssmayr's) is such a discouraging opening for an opera." Here Smith, seemingly convinced that Metastasio, Mazzolà, and Mozart were incompetent dramatists, missed the point that the opening dialogue, declaimed clearly and dynamically in simple recitative, is necessary for an understanding of the duet that follows, and indeed necessary for an understanding of the opera itself, for this dialogue is nothing less than an exposition of its principal issues. By omitting the dialogue Smith completely transformed the scene, robbing Sesto and Vitellia of their characterization and of the motivation behind their actions and their music.

Another cut in the recitative reveals further misunderstanding of the authors' intentions. Tito's soliloquy in which he first signs and then tears up Sesto's death warrant – one of the two scenes in Metastasio's libretto that Voltaire called "comparable to the finest that Greece ever produced" – is nowhere to be found in the 1968 recording. Smith explains: "In order to keep the listener guessing until the very end whether Sesto is to be forgiven or not, and at the same time to save him from several minutes of Süssmayr, we have cut this soliloquy." But Metastasio, Mazzolà, and Mozart wanted the audience to know that Tito was going to pardon Sesto. Without this knowledge we cannot understand the brilliance and exaltation of Tito's last aria, "Se all'impero," in which he celebrates the triumph of clemency. Nor can we experience the irony with which Metastasio colored the subsequent scenes, as all the characters except Tito act in the belief that he has signed the death sentence.

Ponnelle's achievement

The French director Jean-Pierre Ponnelle brought *La clemenza di Tito* to the stage of the Cologne Opera in 1969. That production was the first of a series of productions in which Ponnelle demonstrated to the operatic world the dramatic integrity and power of Mozart's last opera. Ponnelle himself revealed the secret of his success as a director of *Tito* in a discussion about his cycle of Mozart operas at Cologne: he took *Tito* and its characters seriously. Rejecting views typical of the Romantic critical tradition, Ponnelle saw no need to improve or to correct the "masterful score":

It is not the last work of a mortally ill man (who, incidentally, was writing *Zauberflöte* at the same time). Musically I find in *Tito* much that anticipates nineteenth-century opera. For me, educated both at school and at university in close contact with the French classics, the leap from Racine to *Tito* is basically an easy one. I took these characters seriously right away. I am convinced that all of us, even if we are not ourselves Roman emperors, can be interested in their actions and their psychology.[7]

Ponnelle's production in Cologne was just what *Tito* needed: a straightforward presentation of the opera that let it speak for itself. "Ponnelle tackled the opera on its own ground," said Stanley Sadie, "that of 18th-century emotion and 18th-century classicism."[8] Unlike so many directors before him, Ponnelle approached the opera as a viable drama, making the most of what Harold Rosenthal called his "gift of getting his singers to act and, more important, to react, not only to the dramatic but also to the musical situations." The result was a revelation for Rosenthal, who saw the Cologne production when it was presented in London in October 1969. "I never thought I would find it so enjoyable in a stage performance."[9]

During the subsequent decade and a half Ponnelle brought *Tito* to many of the leading operatic centers of Europe and North America, including Salzburg (1976) and New York (1984). His ideas about *Tito* evolved. "I am seven years older than when we did it in Salzburg," said Ponnelle as he prepared his production at the Metropolitan in 1984, "either seven years wiser or else seven years more senile. At any rate, I am not the same now, nor does this opera seem the same."[10] In some of the later productions Ponnelle went beyond the well-balanced restraint of his Cologne production. His characterizations tended to become exaggerated and eccentric. Although Stanley Sadie had nothing but favorable comments about Ponnelle's 1969 production, in which "the emotion of each moment sprang out at us from the stage, carried in every gesture, every movement, in close parallel with the music," he found much to criticize in Ponnelle's production at the Metropolitan Opera fifteen years later. Sadie had no sympathy with Ponnelle's view of Vitellia as a witch-like creature, "who crawls menacingly around the stage trying hard to look evil," and of Tito as "a jumpy neurotic." He also expressed annoyance at another feature of the New York production that became characteristic of Ponnelle's productions of *Tito* – his evocation of Roman (or eighteenth-century?) decadence by the use of crumbling classical architecture in his sets. "I am unsure why the columns looked so time-worn," said Sadie in a parenthesis, "Rome was still quite new in Titus's day."[11]

Much of what was both inspiring and annoying about Ponnelle's productions of *Tito* was brought together in a film version of the opera shown on television in Europe and the United States, and later released as a video-disk.[12] The film, completed in 1980, transferred Ponnelle's Salzburg production to Rome itself. Here Ponnelle was in his element, guiding his characters among the ruins of the Forum and of the Baths of Caracalla (Plate 12). The film was not entirely successful, according to Alan Blyth: "the rather decrepit surroundings and the outdoor setting predictably dwarfed the acting-singers who were further hampered by outlandish 18th-century garments and wigs, which did not in any case march with the antique 'sets.'" Blyth found Ponnelle's characterization of Vitellia ("almost like Lewis Carroll's Queen of Hearts, so bizarre

12   Carol Neblett as Vitellia in Jean-Pierre Ponnelle's film of *Tito* (1980)

was the action she had to cope with") no more convincing than Sadie would a few years later in New York. But he had praise for Ponnelle's "accustomed gift of drawing interior performances from his singers."[13] The fact that the film was made at all was also good reason to praise its director; for no one did more to encourage appreciation for *La clemenza di Tito* than Ponnelle.

Covent Garden, 1974: "This is the *Clemenza di Tito* we have been waiting for."

Few operatic productions have been as influential on the rein-statement of an opera into the standard repertory as was the Covent Garden production of *La clemenza di Tito* in 1974. Anthony Besch directed (he had staged the opera much earlier, when it was presented by the Impresario Society in London in 1957, with the young Heather Harper as Vitellia and Monica Sinclair as Sesto); John Stoddart designed the sets and Colin Davis conducted. The comments of Frank Granville Barker show how closely this production was related to changing opinions of *Tito* in the 1970s:

Considering that *La clemenza di Tito* was the first of Mozart's operas to reach the London stage . . . , it seems incredible that Covent Garden should have waited until now to take it off the shelf for an airing. The trouble no doubt has been that British audiences and critics have an inborn suspicion of opera seria, regarding it as fossilized and untheatrical. After the premiere on April 22, however, it was impossible not to feel that this masterpiece has a good deal more heart and soul than most of the new operas seen in London over the past few years. And the Royal Opera performed it not only with distinction but with love.[14]

(With distinction and with love: how many dozens of eighteenth-century operas, comic and serious alike, could be successfully revived if their productions included these two ingredients!)

Andrew Porter too recognized the Covent Garden production as a turning-point. His review in the *Financial Times* is full of the excitement of discovery; his remarks, like those of Ponnelle quoted above, represent a rejection of the Romantic critical tradition:

In short, this is the *Clemenza di Tito* we have been waiting for, the presentation to prove that Mozart's last opera, so far from being the dull, frigid, alternately short-breathed and long-winded affair that many commentators have deemed it (and some performances might have set out to demonstrate), can be warm, romantic, dramatic, and gripping from first to last . . . *Titus* is revealed as, not a dying man's hurried attempt to fulfil a commission in an uncongenial and dying form, but rather as a landmark in the line of *opera seria* that leads through Spontini, Rossini, and Bellini until it reaches *Aida*.[15]

Porter found much to praise in every aspect of the production. He admired the staging, in which

soloists move naturally and with dignity; . . . a manner that combines directness, and emotional intensity in an individual's predicaments, with firmness of structure, a manner that warms Neo-classical conventions into life, reflects the essential duality of the opera.

Porter found John Stoddart's handsome classical sets to be in a "style that matches the score perfectly." He was delighted with the conducting of Colin Davis, who brought to the music his command of colour, pace, and lyrical intensity ... The orchestral playing – the balancing, the timbres, the shaping of phrases – was very beautiful; it was also dramatic, and so was the pacing of the whole. Mr. Davis is not afraid of a true *adagio*, and he had the singers to sustain it.

The cast was led by Janet Baker in the role of Vitellia. Porter called Baker "the kind of performer who could possibly persuade us that – oh, *Ivanhoe* or *The Queen of Cornwall* is a masterpiece, if she chose; great music becomes incandescent when she sings it." Porter praised the other principals as well: Yvonne Minton was "a strong, exciting Sextus"; Eric Tappy, in the role of Tito, was "a compelling performer who grasps and conveys the sense of the music."

Director and stage designer, conductor and singers together convinced Porter that the Covent Garden production of *Tito* "should literally make history" by causing audiences, singers, and directors to rethink their opinions of *Tito*. This rethinking, Porter implied, would result in a rejection of the view of *Tito* as an unstageworthy opera, a view that had been passed without much rethinking from Jahn to Dent to Anna Amalie Abert. Porter concluded his review with a reference to Abert's comments on *Tito* (cited in chapter 7) in the *New Oxford History of Music*, which had just been published when Porter's review appeared: "Read the account of *Titus* in the newly published Volume VII of the *New Oxford History of Music*; hear and see the Covent Garden production and ask which is the truer account of the piece."

Critical reassessment and new musicological research

The success of Ponnelle's productions of *La clemenza di Tito* and of the Covent Garden production of 1974 affected the way many critics considered the opera. These productions encouraged a re-evaluation of *Tito*, one that involved breaking away from the Romantic critical tradition that had dominated critical response to *Tito* since the middle of the nineteenth century. This reassessment was encouraged too by the publication in 1970 of a new critical edition of *Tito* as part of the *Neue Mozart-Ausgabe*. Another spur to re-evaluation was the article about the origins of *Tito* published by Tomislav Volek in 1959 (to which reference was made in chapter 4). Volek pointed to evidence suggesting that Mozart thought of setting Metastasio's libretto to music as early as 1789, and that he began composing the opera well before Guardasoni signed his contract with the Bohemian Estates on 8 July 1791. One of the claims that critics of *Tito* had rarely failed to make, as we saw in chapter 7, was that Mozart wrote the opera in great haste, in a period of only eighteen days. If *Tito*, instead of being the product of two and a half weeks' hectic labor, had indeed benefitted from Mozart's careful, if intermittent, attention for over a year, it deserved reappraisal.

The reappraisal of *La clemenza di Tito* occurred quickly, so quickly that we find some critics changing their views on the opera within a relatively short time. One such critic was Stanley Sadie, who in his book on Mozart published in 1965 still found *La clemenza di Tito* unsatisfactory. Many of his ideas can be traced back to Ulibishev and Jahn via Hermann Abert and Dent. That *opera seria* was a genre clumsy in its dramaturgy, on the point of dying out in 1791, and hopelessly unsuited to Mozart's approach to dramatic music; that Mozart wrote the opera against his will; that Titus' clemency was exaggerated and unrealistic; that the music contains beautiful things, but that the libretto left Mozart with no chance to create a successful opera: all this is very much in the Romantic critical tradition. For Sadie, *Tito*

was an untimely reversion to Metastasian *opera seria* – untimely because this stiff, static form was totally unsuited to the mature Mozart's dramatic outlook and gifts. In his more prosperous days Mozart would surely have refused to touch a libretto by Metastasio, however skilfully modernised, but in 1791 he was in no position to refuse. The choice of the fifty-seven-year-old text was dictated by political considerations. In the anxious months following the French Revolution it was thought prudent, especially at coronation festivities, to emphasise the wisdom and generosity of monarchs – though Titus' clemency, like the Pasha Selim's, was more than anyone could reasonably believe in.

It is not true to say that *Titus* is musically weak, for it is full of beautiful music of superlative technical craftsmanship. The trouble is that the text effectively killed any possibility of producing a work with real human feeling or dramatic shape.[16]

Even as the American edition of Sadie's book was being readied for publication (1970) his views were evolving. In an essay about *Tito* published in connection with the Cologne Opera's production of the opera in 1969, and in a review of that production, Sadie defended the opera's strengths and expressed his delight and surprise that the opera worked so well on stage. But he still saw grave weaknesses in *Tito*, comparing it unfavorably to the other operas of Mozart's maturity: "*La clemenza di Tito* may seem a strange piece: cool, uneven, in a sense unreal."[17] His own view of the opera was ambivalent: "*La clemenza di Tito* may not be a great work, but the fascination of its ideas is unending to anyone who loves Mozart." No wonder that Sadie's pleasure on seeing the Cologne production was mixed with continued reservations about the opera's quality:

After so much has been said on the musical unevenness and the ineffectual structural mixture of *La clemenza di Tito* – both with complete truth – it was thrilling to discover that the opera could make an evening's entertainment for which no kind of apology is needed.[18]

Sadie revealed his continued allegiance to the Romantic critical tradition by his reference to the opera's "basically weak, unreal plot," and in his discussion of the music and characterization of the title role. His description of Tito's aria "Se all'impero" as "a big, formal showpiece very like the arias of Mozart's youthful operas, complete with vocal roulades and a contrasting middle section" is slightly derogatory in implication. (Recall Dent's remark: "Here is Mozart, definitely in his 'third period', being forced to revert to the style of his first. It was impossible.") Sadie's praise for "Del più sublime soglio," which he considered the best of Tito's three arias, would have been seconded by Jahn, Dent, and Einstein: "there are parallels to it in *Die Zauberflöte* and *Così fan tutte* (perhaps also in Gluck) – this serene tone appears, in fact, in much of Mozart's late music." Having decided that Tito's first aria was his best, Sadie had trouble seeing the emperor's character develop during the drama, as he faced and overcame the challenges of leadership: "It would be too much to expect Titus's character to develop," concluded Sadie, "his clemency is unbounded; he is predictable, and therefore entirely undramatic." Sadie's complaint echoes Jahn's, more than a century old: "The abstract goodness of Titus, who is ready on every occasion to pardon and to yield, rouses no sympathy, and is dramatically mischievous in its effects, since it destroys any sort of suspense."

By 1980, when Sadie's article on Mozart appeared in *The New Grove dictionary*, he had had opportunity to study the opera in its new edition, and to see and hear the opera in several good productions, including that at Covent Garden in 1974. He was much more sure of his admiration for *Tito*:

Until the 1960s, Mozart scholars were inclined to dismiss *La clemenza di Tito* as an opera written hurriedly and with distaste. That it was written hurriedly, even if not as hurriedly as has been supposed, is probably true; but there is no reason to imagine that Mozart had reservations about composing it. Serious opera had always attracted him; and many composers were setting Metastasio's classical librettos modified to meet contemporary taste through the addition of ensembles and choruses...

The opera was composed in a style more austere than that of the Da Ponte operas or *Die Zauberflöte*. This traditionally has been attributed to Mozart's alleged haste; but on other occasions he composed quickly and elaborately, and there is no reason to think that the opera would have been substantially different had he had longer. Its style is appropriate to its topic. The indebtedness of the original Metastasio libretto to French classical models has been pointed out (Moberly, 1974), and in its reduced form it may be seen as conforming to the neo-classical ideals then rapidly gaining ground in Germany. Mozart responded with restrained orchestral writing, smooth, broad vocal lines, and relatively brief numbers.

... *La clemenza di Tito*, compared with the preceding operas, is no less refined in craftsmanship, and it shows Mozart responding with music of restraint, nobility, and warmth to a new kind of stimulus.

Another remarkable conversion is that of the American musicologist and critic Daniel Heartz, who, in his program note for a production of *Idomeneo* at the University of California, Berkeley, in 1969, compared *Idomeneo* to *La clemenza di Tito*, "which is superficially similar as to genre, but which is the product of exhaustion and a commission unworthy of, if not insulting to the composer." Heartz's view, and the somewhat indignant, moralistic tone in which he expressed it, are both products of the Romantic critical tradition; Heartz is particularly indebted to Dent, who preferred *Idomeneo* just as emphatically.

Like Sadie, Heartz changed his opinion quickly during the following years. Indeed Heartz led the way in the critical reappraisal of *La clemenza di Tito* with the publication of several important articles from 1978 on. In the first of these articles Heartz referred to the changes in attitude that had recently occurred, and he pointed to one particular event as a catalyst for the change: during "the last few years," he wrote, *Tito* "has come into its own again, especially with the magnificent production at Covent Garden."[19]

Heartz's articles represented an attack on the Romantic critical tradition along several fronts. He effectively refuted the charge made by Dent that *Tito* is "a rather shapeless opera" by demonstrating its musical coherence. Heartz pointed to the overture, dismissed by Anna Amalie Abert as "a piece of solemn music with no inherent connection with the main body of the opera," as a key to the understanding of *Tito*, a movement in which many of the opera's most important musical features are anticipated. Heartz argued that Mozart, through the use of recurring motives, rhythmic ideas, harmonies, harmonic progressions, and juxtapositions of keys, succeeded in giving the opera a structural integrity that enhances its dramatic power.[20] Developing a point made by Hermann Abert in his revision of Jahn's biography of Mozart, Heartz drew parallels both musical and dramatic between *Tito* and *Die Zauberflöte*. He suggested that *Tito*, far from representing for Mozart "a return to a world whose assumptions had crumbled with those of the *ancien régime* in France two years before" (to use Anna Amalie Abert's words), represents instead much the same philosophy of Masonic benevolence as *Die Zauberflöte*.[21] Heartz refuted the charge commonly made by writers in the Romantic critical tradition that the genre of *opera seria* was dying when Mozart wrote *Tito*, that the opera was an anachronism from the time of its first performance, by showing not only that *opere serie* were being composed and performed in many parts of Europe during the late eighteenth century, but also that *Tito* represents some of the latest developments in the genre. Mozart's aim in writing *Tito*, Heartz argued, was to produce a popular contemporary opera to please contemporary audiences.[22]

In 1976 Don J. Neville made this simple proposition, elegantly summarizing the new view of *Tito*:

> *La clemenza di Tito* is a masterpiece set by its master at the peak of his power as a musical dramatist, to a libretto which gave him the opportunity to draw on his wealth of experience in moulding the forms of the major operatic genres of his short lifetime.[23]

During the decade that followed, Neville produced a series of studies, rich in detail and insight, in which he set out to demonstrate the validity of his view of *La clemenza di Tito*; these studies culminated in a dissertation completed in 1986. He subjected Metastasio's libretto to critical scrutiny, emphasizing its didactic qualities and pointing to ways in which it embodied the moral philosophy of Descartes. He examined Mazzolà's revision and showed how it affected Mozart's musical response to the libretto. His analyses of Mozart's music explored the web of motivic connections linking various parts of the score, thus supplementing and reinforcing Heartz's views on this subject. By dealing sensitively and intelligently with problems of characterization and dramatic structure as articulated by both text and music, Neville contributed much to our understanding of *La clemenza di Tito*.[24]

In order to be able to appreciate *Tito*, an opera in which the libretto, much of it unclothed by Mozart's music, plays such an important role, we need to be able to appreciate the libretto and the conventions that shaped it. The work of several scholars has helped us to do so. R. B. Moberly explored Metastasio's connections with the French dramatists of the seventeenth century;[25] Sergio Durante, presently at work on a major study of *Tito*, has increased our knowledge of late eighteenth-century revisions of Metastasio's librettos.[26]

Another scholar who has devoted much thought to *Tito* is Helga Lühning, who published in 1974 a study of the origins of *Tito* in which she carefully considered the difficult problems of chronology suggested by Volek's pioneering study of 1959. Later Lühning went on to produce a book that explores musical settings of *La clemenza di Tito* from Caldara's original setting of 1734 to the end of the eighteenth century. Focussing on text and music in equal detail, Lühning's book is full of information and ideas about not only Mozart's *Tito* but also eighteenth-century *opera seria* in general.[27]

James Parakilas directed the attention of listeners, scholars, and performers to other aspects of *La clemenza di Tito*. Using the techniques of rhetorical analysis, Parakilas proposed a categorization of arias according to their rhetorical function.[28] For example, the text of the aria "Tu fosti tradito," in which Annio gives Tito advice, is, in terms of the tone of the advice and the shape of the argument, very similar to the text of the aria "Torna di Tito al lato," in which Annio gives advice to Sesto. The similarity in rhetorical content of the texts may help to account for some of the musical similarities between the two arias: moderate tempo (allegretto in the former, andante in the latter), no tempo changes, simple A B A′ structure, lack of coloratura. Vitellia's rondò "Non più di fiori" is of course completely different from these "advice arias" in its rhetorical function; it is a monologue in which the singer communicates directly to the audience rather than to another character; and she communicates emotions rather than advice. This is a mad-scene, closer in its rhetoric to the great mad-scene in Donizetti's *Lucia di Lammermoor* than to Annio's well-meaning sermons. Parakilas pointed to musical similarities between Vitellia's scene and Lucia's, arguing that the two scenes work "on the same principles for representing delirium."[29]

The worlds of operatic scholarship and operatic performance are not isolated from one another, but interconnected and inter-dependent. Just as research into *Tito* was inspired by successful performances of the opera, so performances were influenced by research. Parakilas's imaginative interpretation of "Non più di fiori" soon found its way onto the operatic stage. When *Tito* was performed at Drottningholm in 1987 and 1988, Anita Soldh sang the role of Vitellia with great success, according to Rodney Milnes:

The moment of crisis and resolution, 'Non più di fiori', played as an almost traditional operatic Mad Scene, the woman in picturesque disarray absent-mindedly, obsessively shredding her bridal wreath, made one catch one's breath in terror.[30]

Problems of performance: the challenge of Vitellia and Tito

During the period following the Covent Garden production in 1974 interest in *La clemenza di Tito* on the part of performers as well as scholars has expanded; and the number of good perform-ances has increased dramatically. During the 1980s alone *Tito* was performed in over twenty of the world's operatic centers, of which the following list does not pretend to be exhaustive: Munich, Lud-wigsburg, Hamburg, Bremen, Basel, Geneva, Salzburg, Vienna, Venice, Turin, Paris, Nantes, Aix, Lyon, Brussels, Amsterdam, Drottningholm, London, Birmingham, Edinburgh, New York, Chicago, Seattle, Buenos Aires.

Not all of these productions were equally successful, of course. But an important difference between the way critics reacted to earlier failures and those of the 1980s shows how much critical opinion of *Tito* has changed. Where critics had earlier tended to blame Mozart's opera for weak performances, more often than not they now took the opera's viability for granted and blamed direc-tors and performers for failures.

This was the case, for example, with Joel Kasow's reaction to the production of *Tito* at the Holland Festival in 1983. Kasow called the characters "puppets," just as Einstein had many years earlier. But Einstein was criticizing the characters of Metastasio,

Mazzolà, and Mozart; Kasow was criticizing the characters as performed in Amsterdam:

La clemenza di Tito was rendered insipid by designer-producer Filippo Sanjust, who was content to move his puppets around, unable to convey any notion of the piece to the valiant cast ... Hans Vonk, conducting the Residentie Orchestra, seemed content to slumber along with Mr Sanjust.[31]

As the beauty and strength of *La clemenza di Tito* were recognized by increasing numbers of performers and opera-goers, problems of interpretation and performance became the focus of attention.

To be successful any production of *La clemenza di Tito* needs three first-rate singer-actors for the principal roles, with voices well suited to the particular qualities of the music. Having conquered the technical difficulties posed by the arias and ensembles, these singers have to be able to communicate the complex personalities of the characters they sing – not only in the arias and ensembles, but in the recitative as well.

The role of Vitellia presents challenges that few singers have been able to overcome with complete success. As a singer, the soprano who takes the role of Vitellia must cope with the elaborate coloratura at the end of "Deh se piacer mi vuoi" (Ex. 47); she must be able to cry out in panic the high notes at the end of the trio "Vengo ... aspettate ... Sesto!" (Ex. 48); she must be able to project into the theater her horrified words as she sees Death advancing towards her in "Non più di fiori" (Ex. 49). As an actress, Vitellia must be both wicked and alluring; she must repel us; but we must also be able to understand why Sesto is willing to do so much for her.

Ex. 47

Ex. 48

Ex. 49

Janet Baker triumphed as Vitellia in the 1974 Covent Garden production, according to Frank Granville Barker:

Janet Baker brought out the venom and blackness of the character in a performance of vivid intensity, singing all the lower-lying music with fiery assurance. Although she avoided the top notes – this role almost requires two voices – there was no lack of brilliance in her elaborate "Non più di fiori," with its haunting basset-horn obbligato.[32]

Andrew Porter agreed:

"Non più di fiori" was composed to move without interruption into the final scene, but such an account of it as Janet Baker gave on Monday could hardly pass unapplauded ... She is so bold, so passionate, so delicate. Weight, timbre, line, words are all expressive. She uttered those exclamations – ("Vengo! ... Aspettate! ... Sesto! ... Ahimè!") that begin the trio, the penultimate number of Act 1 – she *acted* them with voice, glance, and gait in a way that made Mozart's Vitellia as vivid as his Elvira.[33]

The highest parts of Vitellia's role strained Baker's voice; she had to leave out the high D in the passage in the trio "Vengo ... aspettate ... Sesto!" quoted above. And in a recording of *La clemenza di Tito* issued in 1977 with Baker in the role of Vitellia, we can hear her straining even in such places as the A near the end of "Non più di fiori."[34] Yet such was Baker's artistry that she could put even the limitations of her voice to dramatic effect, as Porter pointed out, calling Baker's voice "eloquent in the very discolorations of the higher notes."

One of the most successful Vitellias of recent years has been Carol Vaness (Plate 13). She made her professional operatic debut in the role of Vitellia in San Francisco in 1977, and has performed the role many times since, in cities including New York (both City Opera and Metropolitan), London (Covent Garden), Geneva, Paris, and Salzburg. Vaness trained as a mezzo-soprano before changing to soprano roles; in an interview she pointed out that this special background has proven useful in the role of Vitellia:

13   Carol Vaness as Vitellia in Jean-Pierre Ponnelle's production at the Metropolitan Opera, 1987

I was asked to sing Vitellia because having studied as a mezzo I always had a lot of low voice, and then when I worked as a soprano I added the top voice. It's hard to cast Vitellia because it's so wide-ranging and takes a lot of technique. When I was first offered it, people were shocked that I could sing this part, but honestly it's not hard for me, so it can tend to be a bit boring. I've been lucky in that I've had some good conductors who keep my mind going and challenge me musically in the part.[35]

When Vaness sang Vitellia at the Metropolitan Opera in 1987 she impressed Tim Page as a fierce, earthy Vitellia, with a low snarl that provided the evening with an element of visceral drama. Her performance of the rondo showpiece "Non più di fiori" was a tour de force – a minute psychological examination of love and dread.[36]

A year later at the Salzburg Festival she won praise from Horst Koegler:

As Vitellia Carol Vaness lacked perhaps the razor-sharp attack, the vituperative fervour one remembers for instance from Julia Varady's interpretation, but she sang the role with sweeping majesty and with ample, bright soprano resources – and she was the only one occasionally to embark on some appoggiaturas.[37]

When Vaness took up the role of Vitellia at Covent Garden in 1989, her performance was naturally compared to Janet Baker's; from Alan Blyth's reaction we might guess that Vaness had absorbed some of Ponnelle's ideas about Vitellia, perhaps when she sang the role in Ponnelle's production in New York in 1987:

Carol Vaness's view of the jealous, impassioned, frustrated Vitellia was very different from Janet Baker's. She played the part as something of a cross between Callas as Medea and Joan Collins as Alexis [in the American television series "Dynasty"], and who's to say there is much wrong in that? The way she paced the stage, alternately caressed and taunted Sextus, and then became severely guilt-ridden, bespoke a stage creature of a formidable kind. Her singing, full-bodied, lustrous and sensual, was also just right. She did not quite bring to 'Non più di fiori' the variety of dynamics and colour achieved by Baker, but the legato was exemplary, the runs refined. In short, a memorable assumption.[38]

Tito is also a difficult role to bring off, both dramatically and musically. He is a strong, commanding leader; yet he is also generous and gentle. He is firm and resolute; yet subject, like any human being, to the struggle of conflicting values. The singer who must master this subtle and complex role must at the same time be able to sing Tito's arias, the most difficult and important of which is the last, "Se all'impero," with its coloratura and high B-flats.

The difficulty of the role is vividly illustrated by Manfred Schmidt's problems when Ponnelle's Cologne production visited London during October 1969. "Manfred Schmidt just does not seem to have either the vocal technique or the dramatic ability to make anything of Titus," according to Harold Rosenthal. "On the first night he was apparently singing under some kind of difficulty, for he omitted his last-act *bravura* aria: not that he made all that much of it at the performance on October 17."[39]

Kenneth Riegel fell victim to the challenges both of putting the character of Tito across effectively and of singing "Se all'impero," according to Donal Henahan, who heard him sing Tito on the opening night of Ponnelle's production at the Metropolitan in 1984:

Kenneth Riegel's Tito served the purpose when the music did not carry him too high too long. He is not an especially persuasive actor, but he played his part with taste and some sense of the Baroque, Ponnelle style. Vocally, he struggled much of the time and in the famously exhausting "Se all'impero," with its cascading roulades, his tenor came close to giving out.

Eric Tappy, who made his Covent Garden debut as Tito in 1974, was likewise undone by the coloratura of "Se all'impero"; it was his performance that caused Andrew Porter to suggest that tenors "simplify the all but unsingable bars . . . rather than smudge them in a brave attempt." (Tappy continued to have trouble with the aria when he sang the role of Tito the following summer at Aix-en-Provence.) Porter had mixed feelings about Tappy's presentation of Tito's character:

His tenor is not the sweetest around but it is firm, fluent, and true . . . He cut a good figure on the stage but spoilt things a little by jerky, affected waving of his arms and hands. This Titus, like everyone else, was a positive and credible character; the old gibes about instant clemency must stop.

At Drottningholm in 1987 and 1988 Tito was sung by Stefan Dahlberg. Rodney Milnes was impressed, but noted that even Dahlberg could not master all of the roulades: he "sang brilliantly, temporarily defeated only by the passage work in his (very fast) last aria."[40] And in Salzburg in 1988 Gösta Winbergh earned praise for his phrasing and tone from Horst Koegler, but was unable to negotiate some of the coloratura:

Gösta Winbergh's may be a rather light voice for its demands, but he sang his lines with fluency and an iridescent glow, though not without that grainy resilience which his public pronouncements need. Unfortunately he made heavy weather of the coloratura, and 'Se all'impero' found him gasping after Muti's beat.[41]

Even the rare tenor who can meet the technical demands of Tito's last aria may have trouble conveying Tito's character, which involves negotiating a fine line between authority and vulnerability. Stuart Burrows won great praise from Harold Rosenthal for his performance of Tito's arias at Covent Garden ("his breath control was phenomenal and his tone consistently lovely to listen to") and yet at the same time was lightly chastised for presenting Tito as a harsh tyrant rather than a strong but generous monarch: "That he looked more like Nero than Titus hardly seemed to matter."[42]

Tito as political opera

It was argued in Chapter 1 that *La clemenza di Tito*, as performed at Leopold's coronation in 1791, conveyed political messages both to Emperor Leopold, newly crowned as King of Bohemia, and to his subjects. Many directors have sensed the political content of *Tito* and attempted to develop it in performance. Such attempts have not always been successful, because political interpretations have often led directors to stagings that distract audiences from the drama and the music as these were developed by Metastasio, Mazzolà, and Mozart – stagings out of keeping with the spirit of the words and the music.

Sesto appeared "virtually unrecognisable in a sexless combination of greased-back hair and dark suit," according to Andrew Clark, who saw Jean-Claude Auvray's production of *Tito* at Basel in 1984. "The updating illuminated nothing but the stage director's illusions about the work's malleability." Auvray's production presented *Tito* as political allegory, which in itself was to take the opera very much in the spirit in which it was conceived. But Auvray's attempt to portray Tito as a kind of proto-fascist dictator misrepresented the opera's political content, according to Clark;

the parallel between classical and fascist eras was heavily drawn, as ancient Roman figures appeared and disappeared behind reflecting panels of classical architecture and Titus alternated between classical and fascist garb. The rest of the cast were stuck with stylish thirties fashions. Auvray's fundamental mistake was to have overlooked the fact that fascist dictators do not abdicate as in the world dreamed up by the Enlightenment, nor do they grant the kind of 'clemenza' illustrated in any of Mozart's *opere serie*.[43]

Another production dominated by political views that did not seem to fit the opera was Herbert Wernicke's staging in Bremen in 1984. According to Matthias Henneberger and Rein A. Zondergeld, the director's "main concern ... appears to have been not merely to limit an opera to a single aspect, but to expose both the work and its composer: Mozart as the lackey of princes or, more precisely, the representative of an out-dated ideology." In the process of fitting the opera into his ideological framework Wernicke exposed *Tito* "to a considerable amount of ridicule. This, of course, required far-reaching changes in the opera, from cuts in the recitatives, producing a change in the sense, to a final chorus declaiming in Brechtian agit-prop style."

Henneberger and Zondergeld pointed out that the idea of singing the recitatives in German but the arias and ensembles in Italian "emphasised the irrelevance to this production of the emotions expressed in the arias," and they questioned the meaning of some characters' actions, which could not easily be explained even from the point of view of Wernicke's political program. Why, for example, did Servilia and Annio play badminton during the recitative? And why was Sesto to be seen repeatedly dressing and undressing? Despite the uncertainty introduced by such actions, according to Henneberger and Zondergeld,

the final scene removed all doubts as to the (political) message of the production. Far above the stage Tito was enthroned in a golden chair on a white pillar, while the protagonists, no longer in historical costume, became part of the reverential crowd: "The god-ruler and the reverential collective remain" (programme booklet).[44]

Among the more successful political interpretations of *Tito* are those productions that place the opera in the context of eighteenth-century politics and political ideologies rather than those of the twentieth century. One such production was presented in 1987 and 1988 in the beautiful eighteenth-century theater at Drottningholm, near Stockholm. Director Göran Järvefelt developed a connection between Tito's clemency and the enlightened absolutism of eighteenth-century Europe by presenting Tito with the traits of the late eighteenth-century Swedish monarch Gustav III. This gave the opera a new source of irony; for Gustav, like Tito, suffered an assassination attempt; unlike Tito, he succumbed to his attackers. For audiences at Drottningholm the joyful conclusion of *Tito* was tempered with the knowledge that the virtuous emperor before them would soon be assassinated (Plate 14).

The political allegory of *Tito* was evoked on a much grander scale when the opera was performed in Berlin in 1974. Under the direction of Winfried Bauernfeind, the Deutsche Oper Berlin presented *Tito* as an allegory of Habsburg power, with Tito himself represented on stage as the sovereign for whom the opera was written, Leopold II. This production, in other words, explicated or realized some of the allegorical implications of the opera as it was performed in Prague during the French Revolution. As an intro-

14   Stefan Dahlberg as Tito in Göran Järvefelt's production at
Drottningholm, 1987

duction to this world of political allegory, Günter Walbeck provided lavish sets and costumes that placed the action in eighteenth-
century Vienna. Tito's palace was the imperial palace of Schön-
brunn, his audience chamber was the great hall of the court library
in Vienna, the Prunksaal; the Capitol that burned at the end of
Act I was the Karlskirche, built by Leopold's grandfather Emperor
Charles VI (the emperor for whom Metastasio wrote his *La
clemenza di Tito*). The characters wore the clothes and wigs of a
late eighteenth-century emperor and his courtiers. Art and history,
allegory and reality were brought together in this beautiful and
imaginative production.[45]

Aix-en-Provence, 1988: "The triumph of Titus in his clemency"

One recent production of *La clemenza di Tito*, at the summer
festival of Aix-en-Provence in 1988, combined fine singing,
expressive acting, beautiful and appropriate sets and costumes in a
satisfying whole. Critics were almost unanimous in their enthusiasm for the opera and for the staging. The productions of *Tito* in
Cologne in 1969 and London in 1974 can be said to mark the
beginning of the revival of *La clemenza di Tito* as a standard part of
the repertory; as such, they had a somewhat didactic purpose: they

15 David Rendall as Tito and Jeanne Piland as Sesto in Michael
Cacoyannis's production at Aix-en-Provence, 1988

had a point to make, that *Tito* can work on stage; and they made it
well. The Aix production of 1988 can be said to represent a
different kind of achievement: a theatrical experience in which
nothing needed to be proved, but in which every element came
together to produce an unforgettable dramatic experience.

Director Michael Cacoyannis and stage designer Nicholas Georgiadis managed to achieve a beauty of staging rare in productions of
La clemenza di Tito (Plate 15). Charles Pitt, writing in *Opera*,
admired its colors and lighting:

The sumptuous costumes, red for Vitellia, black for Sextus and white for Titus, were set off against a blond sand-coloured background exquisitely lit by Hans Sjoquist. The attractive sets were cleverly designed to give an ongoing pace to the drama. The pillars of Vitellia's apartment pivot round to form the Atrium, then again to form the Capitol with four great rampant horses in the background, then again for Tito's palace with its great imperial doorway.[46]

Pierre-Petit, critic for *Le Figaro*, was equally impressed with the sets, and the atmosphere they established; like Ponnelle, he thought of Racine: "The director has very skillfully drawn the libretto in the direction of classical tragedy, towards a Racinian rigor . . . a refined and timeless classicism.'[47]

Under Cacoyannis's direction the singers avoided the exaggeration, the eccentricity that marred some of Ponnelle's later stagings. David Rendall was a Tito in whom extraordinary virtuosity and skillful acting were united. Rendall "sang with grace, authority and warmth, both on an intimate scale (in 'Del più sublime soglio') and on a more public one ('Se all'impero'),'' according to Stanley Sadie, in *Musical Times*.[48] For Jacques Lonchampt (*Le Monde*) Rendall's interpretation of Tito avoided the dramatic pitfalls that often mar performances of the role:

David Rendall is the most attractive of Titos, no longer the laughingstock, hesitating between vengeance and clemency, that we see only too often, but a just monarch, a faithful friend, deeply hurt, who nevertheless brings about the triumph of the common good, of magnanimity: in short a very Mozartian hero, like the countess in *Figaro*, or like Sarastro.[49]

And Pierre-Petit agreed: "A voice of magnificent fullness, a warm timbre, velvety, seductive, amazing facility in his coloratura, and theatrical intelligence always apparent: he moved us from the moment he entered the stage.''

Vitellia's role, equally complex and difficult, was memorably sung by Charlotte Margiono, who managed, more effectively than most Vitellias, to show the audience how Sesto could be so deeply in love with her. Lonchampt found her "*une Vitellia coquette*, as irresistible and cruel as Alma Mahler, with a luscious, glowing voice.'' According to Pitt she was "just the sort of girl for whom one might set Rome afire.'' At the same time Sadie could admire Margiono's technical abilities as well, praising her as "a tense and powerful Vitellia . . . singing cleanly from the low notes of 'Non più di fiori' to the top D in her alarm during the Act I trio.''

One thing that almost every critic at Aix mentioned was the close relation between the various elements of the production: the beauty of one element called to mind and enhanced the beauty of others. The staging, wrote Sadie,

takes the neo-classicism of the late 18th century as its starting-point, with pillars bearing busts of Roman emperors and costumes that suggested the art of Jacques-Louis David: the cool, restrained style of Mozart's score had an apt visual parallel that gave it extra depth and meaning. The singers responded with a series of readings that beautifully captured the passion underlying this music.

Lonchampt agreed: "The magnificent tone" established by Cacoyannis and Georgiadis in their sets and costumes "is in tune with the refinement of the feelings, the emotions, the gestures of the characters." It was perhaps Lonchampt who expressed most poignantly the feeling that the Aix production of *La clemenza di Tito* achieved a unity of musical and dramatic power rare in any opera, on any stage:

This new production is glorious, stunning and sober, like the triumph of Titus in his clemency; everything has a sublime beauty: sets, lighting, voices, the appearance of the actors, and the orchestra conducted by Armin Jordan like Hans Rosbaud of olden days, like Mozart's music itself.

Notes

1 A coronation opera for the German Titus

1 The crisis of 1789–1790 is discussed in detail by Ernst Wangermann, *From Joseph II to the Jacobin trials*, 2nd edn. (London, 1969), 5–55; see also Robert J. Kerner, *Bohemia in the eighteenth century: a study in political, economic and social history, with special reference to the reign of Leopold II, 1790–1792* (New York, 1932), 82–95, and Adam Wandruszka, *Leopold II*, 2 vols. (Vienna, 1963–65), II, 249–61.

2 On theatrical events in Frankfurt see *Theater-Kalender auf das Jahr 1790* (Gotha, [1790]), 276; on theatrical events in Prague see H. C. Robbins Landon, *1791: Mozart's last year* (London, 1988), 102–21.

3 Kerner, *Bohemia in the eighteenth century*, describes in detail the proceedings of the "Big Bohemian Diet" of 1790–91.

4 The contract is published in Tomislav Volek, "Über den Ursprung von Mozarts Oper 'La clemenza di Tito'," *Mozart-Jahrbuch* 1959, 274–86.

5 Kerner, *Bohemia in the eighteenth century*, 111–12.

6 See the important study by Daniel Heartz, "Mozart and his Italian contemporaries: 'La clemenza di Tito,'" in *Mozart-Jahrbuch* 1978/79, 275–93.

7 Thomas Bauman, *W. A. Mozart: Die Entführung aus dem Serail* (Cambridge, 1987), 18, 124.

8 For the repertory of the Viennese court theaters during the late eighteenth century see Franz Hadamowsky, *Das Wiener Hoftheater (Staatstheater) 1776–1966*, Teil 1: 1776–1810 (Vienna, 1966) and Otto Michtner, *Das alte Burgtheater als Opernbühne von der Einführung des deutschen Singspiels (1778) bis zum Tod Kaiser Leopolds II. (1792)* (Vienna, 1970).

9 On *opera seria* in Florence see Marita McClymonds, "Mozart's *La clemenza di Tito* and opera seria in Florence as a reflection of Leopold II's musical taste," *Mozart-Jahrbuch* 1984/85, 61–70; on Leopold's establishment of an *opera-seria* troupe in Vienna see John A. Rice, "Emperor and impresario: Leopold II and the transformation of Viennese musical theater, 1790–1792", Ph.D. dissertation, University of California, Berkeley, 1987, 254–98.

10 Helga Lühning, Titus-*Vertonungen im 18. Jahrhundert: Untersuchungen zur Tradition der opera seria von Hasse bis Mozart* (*Analecta musicologica* 20 [1983]), 521.

11 Claudio Sartori, manuscript catalogue of Italian librettos in the Biblioteca Braidense, Milan.

12 "Osservazioni sullo spettacolo in generale, sulla tragedia, sulla tragedia domestica-pantomima, sulla commedia, sugli attori, sull'abito scenico, sulle decorazioni, e sugli autori per servire allo stabilimento del nuovo Teatro Nazionale," in Giovanni De Gamerra, *Nuovo teatro*, 18 vols. (Venice, 1790), I, iii, vii, xxvi.

13 According to M. Elizabeth C. Bartlet (personal communication) the earliest version of this anecdote is in André René Polydore Alissan de Chazet, *Mémoires, souvenirs, œuvres et portraits* (Paris, 1837). Bartlet suspects the authenticity of Chazet's account; but there is no doubt that politics played a leading role in the debate over Méhul's *Adrien*. See Bartlet, "On the freedom of the theatre and censorship: the *Adrien* controversy (1792)," forthcoming in the proceedings of the conference "Musique, Histoire, Démocratie" (Paris, July 1989).

14 Adam Wandruszka, "Die 'Clementia Austriaca' und der aufgeklärte Absolutismus: zum politischen und ideelen Hintergrund von 'La clemenza di Tito'," *Österreichische Musikzeitschrift* 31 (1976), 186–93.

15 Francesco Zacchiroli, *Description de la Galerie Royale de Florence*, 3 vols. (Florence, 1783), I, 59; *Gazzetta toscana* 1789, 176 (article dated Livorno, 28 October); *Gazzetta toscana* 1790, 38 (article dated 6 March).

16 Quoted by Erna Berger and Konrad Bund, eds., *Wahl und Krönung Leopolds II. 1790. Brieftagebuch des Feldschers der kursächsischen Schweizergarde* (Frankfurt, 1981), 84.

17 [Joseph Sartori], *Leopoldinische Annalen*, 2 vols. (Augsburg, 1792–93), II, 216 ff. The parallel is quoted in its entirety, in German and English, in John A. Rice, "Political theater in the age of revolution: Mozart's *La clemenza di Tito*," in *Austria in the age of the French Revolution, 1789–1815*, ed. Kinley Brauer and William E. Wright (Minneapolis, 1990), 125–49.

2 Metastasio the romantic

1 For a useful compendium of Arcadian views see Robert S. Freeman, *Opera without drama: currents of change in Italian opera, 1675–1725* (Ann Arbor, 1981), 1–54.

2 Metastasio has been the subject of much interest and research during recent years. Among book-length studies, see Franco Gavazzeni, *Studi Metastasiani* (Padua, 1964), Guido Nicastro, *Metastasio e il teatro del primo settecento* (Rome, 1973), Jacques Joly, *Les fêtes théatrales de Métastase à la cour de Vienne (1731–1767)* (Clermont-Ferrand, 1978), Maria Luisa Astaldi, *Metastasio* (Milan, 1979), Elena Sala Di Felice, *Metastasio: ideologia, drammaturgia, spettacolo* (Milan, 1983), and Gian Piero Maragoni, *Metastasio e la tragedia* (Rome, 1984).

3 On Titus see Brian W. Jones, *The Emperor Titus* (London, 1984), and Hermann Bengtson, *Die Flavier: Vespasian, Titus, Domitian* (Munich, 1979), 155–78.

4 Jones, *The Emperor Titus*, 114–57.

5 Gaius Suetonius Tranquillus, *The twelve Caesars*, trans. Robert Graves (Baltimore, 1957), 292.
6 Helga Lühning, Titus-*Vertonungen im 18. Jahrhundert: Untersuchungen zur Tradition der opera seria von Hasse bis Mozart* (*Analecta musicologica* 20 [1983]), 16.
7 Robert B. Moberly, "The influence of French classical drama on Mozart's *La clemenza di Tito*," *Music and Letters* (1974), 286–98.
8 Throughout this chapter *La clemenza di Tito* refers to Metastasio's original libretto, which is quoted from its first edition (Vienna, 1734).
9 Freeman, *Opera without drama*, 178–96.
10 *Ibid.*, 254.
11 Vernon Lee (pseudonym of Violet Paget), *Studies of the eighteenth century in Italy*, 2nd. edn. (London, 1907), 294.
12 *Ibid.*, 298.
13 *Ibid.*, 299–300.

3 Mazzolà's revision

1 Mazzolà's revisions have been the subject of several studies: Franz Giegling, "Metastasios Oper 'La clemenza di Tito' in der Bearbeitung durch Mazzolà," *Mozart-Jahrbuch* 1968/70, 88–94; Don J. Neville, "*La clemenza di Tito*: Metastasio, Mazzolà and Mozart," *Studies in Music from the University of Western Ontario* 1 (1976), 124–48; Walther Dürr, "Zur Dramaturgie des 'Titus': Mozarts libretto und Metastasio," *Mozart-Jahrbuch* 1978/79, 55–61; Helga Lühning, Titus-*Vertonungen im 18. Jahrhundert: Untersuchungen zur Tradition der opera seria von Hasse bis Mozart* (*Analecta musicologica* 20 [1983]), 79–108.
2 On Mazzolà's career see Maria Calzavara in Mazzolà, *Caterino Mazzolà: poeta teatrale alla corte di Dresda dal 1780 al 1796* (Rome, 1964).
3 Mazzolà's service to the Burgtheater is recorded in the theater payment records in Vienna's Haus-, Hof-, und Staatsarchiv, Generalintendanz der Hoftheater (Rechnungsbücher, 1791), 36.
4 Sergio Durante, "Matters of taste and dramatic pace in Metastasian revisions for Florence (*c.* 1785–95)," paper given at, and forthcoming in the proceedings of, the conference "Patrons, Politics, Music and Art: Italy 1750–1850," University of Louisville, Louisville, Kentucky, March 1989.
5 On Paisiello's *Pirro* and its use of the *introduzione* and finale see Daniel Heartz, "Mozart and his Italian contemporaries: 'La clemenza di Tito'," in *Mozart-Jahrbuch* 1978/79, 275–93.
6 Alfred Einstein, *Mozart: his character, his work*, trans. by Arthur Mendel and Nathan Broder (New York, 1945), 410.
7 *La dama soldato*, dramma giocoso per musica (Dresden, 1791), 142–46.
8 The libretto printed for the first production of Mozart's *La clemenza di Tito* (Prague, 1791) reverses the order of the first two lines and replaces "tronchi" with "tolga." But the original order (that is, the order in which lines appear in the libretto of *La dama soldato*) and the word

"tronchi" are to be found in Mozart's autograph and consequently in the edition of *La clemenza di Tito* in the *Neue Mozart-Ausgabe*.

9 Vernon Lee, *Studies in the eighteenth century in Italy*, 2nd edn. (London, 1907), 347.

10 For a fine study of Brutus as a political symbol see Robert L. Herbert, *David, Voltaire*, Brutus *and the French Revolution: an essay in art and politics* (London, 1972).

4 Composition and first performance

1 The letter is published, with English translation and commentary, in "Acta musicalia," *Haydn Yearbook* 15 (1984), 153–57; the English translation appears again in H. C. Robbins Landon, *1791: Mozart's last year* (London, 1988), 86–87; I have followed that translation with the exception of one crucial passage in Salieri's original, "l'Impressario di Praga è stato cinque volte da me," which is mistranslated in the *Haydn Yearbook* and Landon: "the impresario came five times from Prague to Vienna."

2 Mozart to his father, 4 February 1778, *Mozart: Briefe und Aufzeichnungen*, Wilhelm A. Bauer, Otto Erich Deutsch, and Joseph Heinz Eibl, eds., 7 vols. (Kassel, 1962–75), II, 251–54.

3 Mozart to Archduke Francis, *Mozart: Briefe und Aufzeichnungen* IV, 107; facsimile opposite p. 112.

4 Leopold Mozart to Lorenz Hagenauer, 16 October 1762, *Mozart: Briefe und Aufzeichnungen* I, 50–53.

5 Leopold Mozart to his wife, 3 April 1770, *Mozart: Briefe und Aufzeichnungen* I, 330–32.

6 *Ibid.*, 9 January 1773, 474–76.

7 *Ibid.*, 23 January 1773, 476–77; see Wolfgang Amadeus Mozart, *Lucio Silla*, ed. Kathleen Hansell (Neue Ausgabe Sämtlicher Werke) (Kassel, 1986), xxxii–xxxiii.

8 Alan Tyson, "'La clemenza di Tito' and its chronology," in *Musical Times* 116 (1975), 221–27, reprinted in *Mozart: studies of the autograph scores* (Cambridge, Mass., 1987), 48–60.

9 Tomislav Volek, "Über den Ursprung von Mozarts Oper 'La clemenza di Tito,'" *Mozart-Jahrbuch* 1959, 274–86.

10 Some further evidence in favor of Volek's argument can be adduced. The similarities in style and imagery between the first quatrain of "Non più di fiori" and the following lines in Mazzolà's libretto *Elisa*, a *dramma per musica* set to music by Naumann and performed in Dresden in 1781, suggest that Mazzolà could easily have provided Mozart with the text for "Non più di fiori": "Son dolci d'Imene / Le fiamme, gli ardori: / Di lui le catene / Son fatte di fiori..." (The flames and passions of Hymen are sweet: his chains are made of flowers.) If Mazzolà did indeed write the text of "Non più di fiori," it would be likely that he and Mozart were already in collaboration on *La clemenza di Tito* by April 1791.

11 *Gazzetta urbana veneta* 1790, 657 (letter dated Padua, 11 October).

12 *Ibid.*, 445 (letter dated Brescia, 5 August).

13 Extract of a letter from Reichardt to the singer Ludwig Fischer, *Berlinische musikalische Zeitung*, 1793, 10 (23 February).

14 *Berlinische musikalische Zeitung*, 1793, 2 (9 February).

15 Claudio Sartori, manuscript catalogue of Italian opera librettos, Biblioteca Braidense, Milan.

16 William Beckford, *Dreams, waking thoughts and incidents*, ed. Robert J. Gemmett (Rutherford, New Jersey, 1971), 174–75. I am grateful to Daniel Heartz for pointing out this reference to Bedini.

17 *Gazzetta urbana veneta* 1791, 384 (letter dated Padua, 15 June).

18 The career of Prospero Braghetti, who started out in the mid-1770s in Italy singing tenor roles in comic opera, is a case in point. Braghetti was originally hired by Haydn's employer Prince Nicholas Esterhazy to sing comic opera, but when the Prince added *opera seria* to the repertory at Esterhaza in 1783 Braghetti became a mainstay of *opera seria* productions as well, often singing the *primo uomo* role transposed down an octave. He later continued his career in London, and there too he sang in both comic and serious opera. Braghetti was still singing in London in 1806, when *La clemenza di Tito* reached the London stage; he sang Annio, that part, like Sesto's, having been turned into a tenor role.

19 In Ferrando's role we see Mozart treating Calvesi's voice differently from the way he treated Baglioni's. Gs and As above middle C are much more common than in Baglioni's music. In the aria "Tradito, schernito" we find G sustained in much the same way that F is sustained in "Il mio tesoro." At the end of the trio "Una bella serenata," Calvesi had to sing half-notes A and G at the final cadence, and he had to sing them forcefully, since he was competing not only with Guglielmo and Alfonso, but also with an orchestra (including trumpets and drums) playing *forte*. In the aria "Ah lo veggio," which Mozart decided to cut from performances of *Così fan tutte*, he gave Calvesi many high B flats to sing.

20 Quoted by Christopher Raeburn, "Mozarts Opern in Prag," in *Musica* XIII (1959), 158–63. The passage is attributed to Niemetschek and quoted in translation in Landon, *1791: Mozart's last year*, 109–10.

21 On Stadler, his instruments, and the music Mozart wrote for him see George Dazeley, "The original text of Mozart's Clarinet Concerto," in *Music Review* 9 (1948), 166–72; M. Kingdon-Ward, "Mozart's clarinettist," in *Monthly Musical Record* 85 (1955), 8–14; Ernst Hess, "Die ursprüngliche Gestalt des Klarinettenkonzertes KV 622," in *Mozart-Jahrbuch* 1967, 18–30; and Alan Hacker, "Mozart and the basset-clarinet," in *Musical Times* 110 (1969), 359–62.

22 Landon, *1791: Mozart's last year*, 102–12.

23 Otto Erich Deutsch, ed., *Mozart: Die Dokumente seines Lebens* (Kassel, 1961), 380.

24 *Mozart: Briefe und Aufzeichnungen*, IV, 154.

25 Jiří Hilmera, "The theatre of Mozart's *Don Giovanni*," in *Mozart's Don Giovanni in Prague*, (Prague, 1987), 11–20.

26 *Prager Oberpostamtszeitung*, 6 September 1791, as cited in *Mozart: Die Dokumente seines Lebens*, 524. According to Deutsch the phrase "einige tausend" means "more than a thousand."

27 These measurements are approximate. They are derived from the engravings illustrated in Hilmera, "The theatre of Mozart's *Don Giovanni*," 14–17, with the assumption that 1 *Wiener Klafter* (1 Viennese fathom) equals 1.8 meters.

28 Hilmera, "The theatre of Mozart's *Don Giovanni*," 18.

29 This passage is reproduced in facsimile and transcribed in Joseph Heinz Eibl, "'. . . Una porcheria tedesca?' Zur Uraufführung von Mozarts 'La clemenza di Tito,'" in *Österreichische Musikzeitschrift* 31 (1976), 332–33.

30 Eibl, "'. . . Una porcheria tedesca'?", 331 cites this statement in Alfred Meissner's *Rococobilder* (Gumbinnen, 1871, 141): "The Emperor spoke contemptuously [about the opera] and the Empress called the music a porcheria tedesca." Meissner's grandfather, on whose notes the book was based, was August Gottlieb Meissner, the poet who supplied the text for a coronation cantata performed in Prague's National Theater on 12 September 1791, less than a week after the premiere of *La clemenza di Tito*. A. G. Meissner could thus have been a reliable source. But Eibl points out that the fourth volume of Otto Jahn's biography of Mozart, which appeared in 1859, well before Alfred Meissner's book, contains some of the same words: "In Prague the tradition has been preserved that the Empress spoke contemputously about the *porcheria* of German music." Eibl concludes that although Alfred Meissner could have found the expression "porcheria tedesca" among the papers of his grandfather, he could also have been paraphrasing Jahn or quoting from some other nineteenth-century source, perhaps the one that Jahn used.

31 "au soir au Theatre la grande opera n'est pas grande chose et la musique très mauvaise ainsi nous y avons presque tous dormi. Le Couronnement est allé a merveille." Vienna, Haus-, Hof- und Staatsarchiv, Sammelbände, Karton 52.

32 Volek, "Über den Ursprung von Mozarts Oper 'La clemenza di Tito,'" 284–85.

33 Quoted by Christopher Raeburn, "Mozarts Opern in Prag," in *Musica* 13 (1959), 158–63. The passage is attributed to Niemetschek and quoted in translation in Landon, *1791: Mozart's last year*, 117–18.

34 *Mozart: Die Dokumente seines Lebens*, 524–25.

35 Mozart to his wife, 7–8 October 1791, *Mozart: Briefe und Aufzeichnungen*, IV, 157–59.

5 Synopsis and commentary

1 Daniel Heartz, "Mozart's overture to *Titus* as dramatic argument," in *Musical Quarterly* 64 (1978), 29–49.

2 Erik Smith, program notes for recording of *La clemenza di Tito*, London OSA 1387 (1968).

3 See, for example, Robert B. Moberly and Christopher Raeburn, "The Mozart version of *La clemenza di Tito*," *Music Review* 31 (1970), 285–94.

4 Helga Lühning, Titus-*Vertonungen im 18. Jahrhundert: Unter-*

suchungen zur Tradition der opera seria von Hasse bis Mozart (*Analecta musicologica* 20 [1983]), 322–26.

5 Hermann Abert, *W. A. Mozart*, 2nd ed. (Leipzig, 1923–24), II, 735.

6 Daniel Heartz, "La clemenza di Sarastro: Masonic benevolence in Mozart's last operas," in *Musical Times* 124 (1983), 152–57.

7 Metastasio seems to have adapted these lines from the Greek historian Dio Cassius, who reported that Titus made the following statement: "It is impossible for me to be insulted or abused in any way, for I do nothing that deserves censure and I care nothing for what is reported falsely." Quoted in translation by Brian W. Jones, *The Emperor Titus* (London, 1984), 115.

8 "This recitative is the longest and most tedious in the entire opera." Don J. Neville, "*Idomeneo* and *La clemenza di Tito*: opera seria and 'vera opera,'" in *Studies in Music from the University of Western Ontario* 3 (1978), 112.

9 *Lettere capricciose di Francesco Albergati Capacelli e di Francesco Zacchiroli dai medesimi capricciosamente stampate*, Venice 1780–81; quoted in John A. Rice, "Sense, sensibility, and opera seria: an epistolary debate," in *Studi musicali* 15 (1986), 101–3.

10 Andrew Porter, review of the production of *Tito* at Covent Garden, *Financial Times*, 24 April 1974.

11 "Mozart's mad scene," in *Soundings* 10 (1983), 3–17.

6 *Tito* in performance, 1791–1850

1 Edward Dent, *Mozart's operas* (London, 1913), 316; 2nd. edn. (London, 1947), 212.

2 Otto Erich Deutsch, ed., *Mozart: Die Dokumente seines Lebens* (Kassel, 1961), 380.

3 Alfred Loewenberg, *Annals of opera, 1597–1940*, 3rd edn. (Totowa, New Jersey, 1978), cols. 491–99.

4 *Mozart: Dokumente*, 412–13.

5 *Mozart: Dokumente*, 415.

6 *Mozart: Dokumente*, 416.

7 *Mozart: Dokumente*, 416–17.

8 *Mozart: Dokumente*, 527–28.

9 *Mozart: Dokumente*, 420–21.

10 Loewenberg, *Annals of opera, 1597–1940*, cols. 491–93.

11 *Allgemeine musikalische Zeitung* (hereafter referred to as *AMZ*) 11 (1808–9), col. 454.

12 *AMZ* 6 (1803–4), cols. 504–6.

13 *AMZ* 13 (1811), cols. 145–46.

14 *AMZ* 6 (1803–4), cols. 504–6.

15 *AMZ* 18 (1816), col. 268.

16 *AMZ* 12 (1809–10), cols. 675–76.

17 *AMZ* 11 (1808–9), cols. 297–98.

18 *AMZ* 2 (1799–1800), col. 48–49.

19 Albert Köster, ed., *Die Briefe der Frau Rath Goethe*, 2 vols. (Leipzig, 1904), II, 73–75.

20 Richard, Earl of Mount Edgcumbe, *Musical reminiscences, containing an account of the Italian opera in England, from 1773*, 4th edn. (London, 1834), 119–21.

21 *Ibid.*, 121–22.

22 *Ibid.*, 125.

23 W. T. Parke, *Musical memoirs, comprising an account of the general state of music in England from the first Commemoration of Handel, in 1784, to the year 1829*, 2 vols. (London, 1830), II, 3–4.

24 *Daily Advertiser*, 28 March 1806, quoted by William C. Smith, *The Italian opera and contemporary ballet in London, 1789–1820* (London, 1955), 80.

25 Mount Edgcumbe, *Musical reminiscences*, 100.

26 *Morning Chronicle*, 4 March 1816, quoted by Smith, *The Italian opera*, 137.

27 *AMZ* 48 (1846), cols. 24–26.

28 Mount Edgcumbe, *Musical reminiscences*, 132.

7 The Romantic critical tradition

1 Franz Xaver Niemetschek, *Leben des K. K. Kapellmeisters Wolfgang Gottlieb Mozart, nach Originalquellen beschrieben* (Prague, 1798), 73.

2 Richard Wagner, "Über die Anwendung der Musik auf das Drama" (1879), in *Richard Wagner: Dichtungen und Schriften*, ed. Dieter Borchmeyer, 10 vols. (Frankfurt am Main, 1983), IX, 327.

3 Wagner, *Oper und Drama*, in *Richard Wagner: Dichtungen und Schriften*, VII, 38.

4 Alexandre Oulibicheff [Alexander Dmitryevich Ulibishev], *Nouvelle biographie de Mozart*, 3 vols. (Moscow, 1843), III, 375–95.

5 Otto Jahn, *W. A. Mozart*, cited here in translation by Pauline D. Townsend, 3 vols. (London, 1882), III, 290–302.

6 Edward J. Dent, *Mozart's operas: a critical study*, 2nd edn. (London, 1947), 212–15.

7 Alfred Einstein, *Mozart: his character, his work* (New York, 1945), 407–11.

8 "This idea must have been entirely Mozart's own invention," according to Dent, because the chorus sings nothing but the word "Ah" until considerably later in the finale. But Dent did not mention that the soloists hear and respond to the chorus ("Le gride, ahimè, ch'io sento / Mi fan gelar d'orror"), and these lines rhyme with another two-line unit within the finale ("Di questo tradimento / Chi mai sarà l'autor?") Unless we are prepared to assign all this poetry to Mozart, it is difficult to credit him with the idea of choral entry on "Ah."

9 "Verbürgte Anekdoten aus Wolfgang Gottlieb Mozarts Leben," *Allgemeine musikalische Zeitung* 1 (1798–99), several installments from col. 17 (for the passage quoted here see cols. 151–52).

10 Joseph Kerman, *Opera as drama*, 2nd. edn. (Berkeley, 1988).

11 Anna Amalie Abert, "The operas of Mozart," *The New Oxford history of music*, VII (London, 1973), 97–172.

8 Performance and critical re-evaluation since 1949

1 *Opera News* 17 (1952), No. 2, 11–13.
2 *New York Times*, 5 August 1952.
3 *Herald Tribune*, 6 August 1952.
4 *Opera* 18 (1967), 920–21.
5 *New York Times*, 23 January 1971.
6 Erik Smith, program notes for recording of *La clemenza di Tito*, London OSA 1387 (1968).
7 "Mozart total: Gedankensplitter von Jean-Pierre Ponnelle zu seinem Kölner Mozart-Zyklus," *Opernwelt* 1975, No. 8, 39.
8 *Musical Times*, 110 (1969), 1266–67.
9 *Opera* 20 (1969), 1093–96.
10 Bernard Holland, "A neglected Mozart opera makes its debut at the Metropolitan," *New York Times*, 14 October 1984.
11 *Musical Times* 126 (1985), 42.
12 Deutsche Grammophon 072 507–1 (CD Video released in 1989).
13 *Opera* 32 (1981), 970–72.
14 *Opera News* 39 (1974), No. 2, 26.
15 *Financial Times*, 24 April 1974.
16 Stanley Sadie, *Mozart* (London, 1965), 160.
17 Stanley Sadie, "Mozart's last opera," in *Opera* 20 (1969), 837–43.
18 *Musical Times*, 110 (1969), 1266–67.
19 Daniel Heartz, "Mozart's overture to *Titus* as dramatic argument," *Musical Quarterly* 64 (1978), 30.
20 "Mozart's overture to *Titus* as dramatic argument," in *Musical Quarterly* 64 (1978), 29–49.
21 "La clemenza di Sarastro: Masonic benevolence in Mozart's last operas," in *Musical Times* 124 (1983), 1523–57.
22 "Mozart and his Italian contemporaries: 'La clemenza di Tito,'" in *Mozart-Jahrbuch* (1978–79), 275–93.
23 Don J. Neville, "*La clemenza di Tito*: Metastasio, Mazzolà and Mozart," *Studies in music from the University of Western Ontario* 1 (1976), 146.
24 Don J. Neville, "*Idomeneo* and *La clemenza di Tito*: opera seria and 'vera opera,'", in *Studies in music from the University of Western Ontario* 2 (1977), 136–66; 3 (1978), 97–126; 5 (1980), 99–121; 6 (1981), 112–46; 8 (1983), 107–36; 10 (1985), 25–49; and "Cartesian principles in Mozart's *La clemenza di Tito*," in *Studies in the History of Music* 2 (1988), 97–123.
25 R. B. Moberly, "The influence of French classical drama on Mozart's *La clemenza di Tito*," *Music and Letters* 55 (1974), 286–93.
26 Sergio Durante, "Matters of taste and dramatic pace in Metastasian revisions for Florence (*c.* 1785–95)," paper given at, and forthcoming in the proceedings of, the conference "Patrons, politics, music, and art: Italy 1750–1850," University of Louisville, Louisville, Kentucky, March 1989.
27 Helga Lühning, "Zur Entstehungsgeschichte von Mozarts 'Titus,'" in *Musikforschung* 27 (1974), 300–18; Titus-*Vertonungen im 18.*

Jahrhundert: Untersuchungen zur Tradition der opera seria von Hasse bis Mozart (Analecta musicologica 20 [1983]).

28 James Parakilas, "Mozart's *Tito* and the music of rhetorical strategy," Ph.D. dissertation, Cornell University, 1979.
29 James Parakilas, "Mozart's mad scene," in *Soundings* 10 (1983), 3–17.
30 *Opera* 39 (1988), Festival Issue, 13.
31 *Opera* 34 (1983), Festival Issue, 100.
32 *Opera News* 39 (1974), No. 2, 26.
33 *Financial Times*, 24 April 1974.
34 Philips 6703.079.
35 Elizabeth Forbes, "Carol Vaness," *Opera* 40 (1989), 418–24.
36 *New York Times*, 24 January 1987.
37 *Opera* 39 (1988), Festival Issue, 44–46.
38 *Opera* 40 (1989), 739–41.
39 *Opera* 20 (1969), 1093–96.
40 *Opera* 38 (1987), 1299.
41 *Opera* 39 (1988), Festival Issue, 44–46.
42 *Opera* 34 (1983), 1264–66.
43 *Opera* 35 (1984), 1035–38.
44 *Opera* 35 (1984), 1140–42.
45 See Sybill Mahlke, "Mozarts 'Titus' in der Deutschen Oper Berlin," *Opernwelt* (1974), No. 12, 21–22, and Winfried Bauernfeind, "Titus – eine Allegorie auf die Habsburger," *Opernwelt* (1974), No. 12, 23.
46 *Opera* 39 (1988), Festival Issue, 56.
47 *Le Figaro*, 12 July 1988.
48 *Musical Times* 129 (1988), 550–51.
49 *Le Monde*, 17–18 July, 1988.

Bibliography

Abert, Anna Amalie, "The operas of Mozart," *The new Oxford history of music*, 11 volumes projected, VII (London, 1973), 97–172

"Mozarts italianità in *Idomeneo* und *Titus*", *Analecta musicologica* 18 (1978), 205–16

Abert, Hermann, *W. A. Mozart* [revision of Otto Jahn, *W. A. Mozart*], 2 vols. (Leipzig, 1919–21; 2nd edn. 1923–24; 3rd edn. 1955–56; 4th edn. 1973–75; 5th edn. 1978)

Angermüller, Rudolph, *Mozart: Die Opern von der Uraufführung bis heute* (Frankfurt am Main, 1988)

Bauer, Wilhelm A., and Otto Erich Deutsch, eds. *Mozart: Briefe und Aufzeichnungen, Gesamtausgabe*, 4 vols. with 2 vols. commentary and 1 vol. index (Kassel, 1962–75)

Beránek, Jiří, "K otáczce hudební složky českých korunovačnich slavností v roce 1791" (Concerning the musical components of the Bohemian coronation festivites in 1791), *Miscellanea musicologica* 30 (1983), 81–113

Binni, Walter, *L'Arcadia e il Metastasio* (Florence, 1963)

Brophy, B., "Pro 'Tito,'" *Musical Times* 110 (1969), 600–607

Calzavara in Mazzolà, Maria, *Caterino Mazzolà: poeta teatrale alla corte di Dresda dal 1780 al 1796* (Rome, 1964)

Camerini, Silvia, ed., *La clemenza di Tito* [program book for production of *La clemenza di Tito* at Teatro Comunale di Bologna, with articles by Piero Buscaroli, Bruno Brizi and Giorgio Gualerzi, and a complete libretto] (Bologna, 1988)

Dent, Edward J., *Mozart's operas: a critical study* (London, 1913; 2nd edn. 1947)

Deutsch, Otto Erich, ed., *Mozart: Die Dokumente seines Lebens*, Neue Mozart-Ausgabe Series 10: Supplement, Work-group 34 (Kassel, 1961) [In English, with additions: *Mozart: A documentary biography*, trans. Eric Blom, Peter Branscombe, and Jeremy Noble (Stanford, 1965)]

Downes, Edward, "*Secco* recitative in early classical *opera seria* (1720–80)," in *Journal of the American Musicological Society* 14 (1961), 50–69.

Durante, Sergio, "Matters of taste and dramatic pace in Metastasian revisions for Florence (ca. 1785–95)" [paper given at, and forthcoming in the proceedings of, the conference "Patrons, politics, music and art: Italy 1750–1850," University of Louisville, Louisville, Kentucky, March 1989]

Dürr, Walther, "Zur Dramaturgie des 'Titus': Mozarts libretto und Metastasio," in *Mozart-Jahrbuch* 1978/79, 55–61

Eibl, Joseph Heinz, "'. . . Una porcheria tedesca?' Zur Uraufführung von Mozarts 'La clemenza di Tito,'" in *Österreichische Musikzeitschrift* 31 (1976), 329–34

Einstein, Alfred, *Mozart: his character, his work*, trans. Arthur Mendel and Nathan Broder (New York, 1945)

Floros, Constantin, "Das 'Programm' in Mozarts Meisterouvertüren," *Studien zur Musikwissenschaft* 26 (1964), 140–86 [reprinted with minor changes in his *Mozart-Studien I: Zu Mozarts Sinfonik, Opern– und Kirchenmusik* (Wiesbaden, 1979)]

Giegling, Franz, "Zu den Rezitativen von Mozarts Oper 'Titus'," *Mozart-Jahrbuch* 1967, 121–26

"Metastasios Oper 'La clemenza di Tito' in der Bearbeitung durch Mazzolà," *Mozart-Jahrbuch* 1968/70, 88–94

"'La clemenza di Tito': Metastasio, Mazzolà, Mozart," *Österreichische Musikzeitschrift* 31 (1976), 321–29

Heartz, Daniel, "Mozart's overture to *Titus* as dramatic argument," *Musical Quarterly* 64 (1978), 29–49

"Mozart and his Italian contemporaries: 'La clemenza di Tito,'" *Mozart-Jahrbuch* 1978/79, 275–93

"Mozarts 'Titus' und die italienische Oper um 1800," *Hamburger Jahrbuch für Musikwissenschaft* 5 (1981), 255–66

"La clemenza di Sarastro: Masonic benevolence in Mozart's last operas," in *Musical Times* 124 (1983), 152–57

Herbert, Robert L., *David, Voltaire*, Brutus *and the French Revolution: an essay in art and politics* (London, 1972)

Hildesheimer, Wolfgang, *Mozart* (Frankfurt, 1977), trans. Marion Faber (New York, 1982)

Jahn, Otto, *W. A. Mozart*, 4 vols. (Leipzig, 1856–59; 2nd edn, 2 vols. Leipzig, 1867; 3rd ed. revised by Hermann Dieters, Leipzig, 1889–91, 4th edn. Leipzig, 1905–1907; 5th edn. revised by Hermann Abert, Leipzig, 1919–21 [see Abert]), trans. Pauline D. Townsend, 3 vols. (London, 1882)

Jones, Brian W., *The Emperor Titus* (London, 1984)

Kunze, Stefan, *Mozarts Opern* (Stuttgart, 1984)

Kerman, Joseph, *Opera as drama* (New York, 1956; 2nd edn. Berkeley, 1988)

Kerner, Robert J., *Bohemia in the eighteenth century: A study in political, economic and social history, with special reference to the reign of Leopold II, 1790–1792* (New York, 1932)

Landon, H. C. Robbins, *1791: Mozart's last year* (London 1988)

Lee, Vernon (Pseudonym of Violet Paget), *Studies of the eighteenth century in Italy*, 2nd. edn. (London, 1907)

Lühning, Helga, "Zur Entstehungsgeschichte von Mozarts 'Titus,'" in *Die Musikforschung* 27 (1974), 300–318

"Mozarts 'Titus' – zwischen Krönungsoper und musikalischem Drama," program note to recording of *La clemenza di Tito*, Deutsche Grammophon 2709 092 (1979)

"Die Rondo-Arie im späten 18. Jahrhundert: Dramatischer Gehalt und musikalischer Bau," *Hamburger Jahrbuch für Musikwissenschaft* 5 (1981), 219–46

Titus-Vertonungen im 18. Jahrhundert: Untersuchungen zur Tradition der opera seria von Hasse bis Mozart, Analecta musicologica 20 (1983)

Mann, William, *The operas of Mozart* (London, 1977)

McClymonds, Marita, "Mozart's *La clemenza di Tito* and *opera seria* in Florence as a reflection of Leopold II's musical taste," *Mozart-Jahrbuch* 1984–85, 61–70

Moberly, Robert B., "The influence of French classical drama on Mozart's 'La clemenza di Tito'," *Music and letters* 55 (1974), 286–98

Moberly, Robert B. and Raeburn, Christopher, "The Mozart version of *La clemenza di Tito*," *Music Review* 31 (1970), 285–95

Mojsisovics, R. von, "Mozarts *Titus* als 'opera buffa,'" *Neue Zeitschrift für Musik* 102 (1935), 1015

Mount Edgcumbe, Richard, Earl of, *Musical reminiscences, containing an account of the Italian Opera in England, from 1773*, 4th ed. (London, 1834)

Nettl, Paul, *Mozart in Böhmen* (Prague, 1938)

"Prager Mozartiana," *Mitteilungen der Internationalen Stiftung Mozarteum* 9 (1960), Nos. 3–4, 4.

Neville, Don J., "*La clemenza di Tito*: Metastasio, Mazzolà and Mozart," *Studies in music from the University of Western Ontario* 1 (1976), 124–48

"*Idomeneo* and *La clemenza di Tito*: opera seria and 'vera opera,'" *Studies in music from the University of Western Ontario* 2 (1977), 138–66, 3 (1978), 97–126, 5 (1980), 99–121, 6 (1981) 112–46, 8 (1983), 107–36, 10 (1985), 25–49

"Moral philosophy in Metastasian dramas," *Studies in music from the University of Western Ontario* 7 (1982), 28–46

"Mozart's *La clemenza di Tito* and the Metastasian *opera seria*," Ph.D. dissertation, Cambridge University, 1986

"Cartesian principles in Mozart's *La clemenza di Tito*," *Studies in the history of music* 2 (1988), 97–123

Niemetschek, Franz Xaver, *Leben des K. K. Kapellmeisters Wolfgang Gottlieb Mozart, nach Originalquellen beschrieben* (Prague, 1798)

Nissen, George Nikolaus von, *Biographie W. A. Mozarts*, ed. Constanze von Nissen (Leipzig, 1828)

Osborne, Charles, *The complete operas of Mozart: a critical guide* (New York, 1978)

Oulibicheff, Alexandre [Alexander Dmitryevich Ulibishev], *Nouvelle biographie de Mozart*, 3 vols. (Moscow, 1843)

Parakilas, James, "Mozart's *Tito* and the music of rhetorical strategy," Ph.D. dissertation, Cornell University 1979

"Mozart's mad-scene" [on "Non più di fiori"], *Soundings* 10 (1983), 3–17

Paumgartner, Bernhard, "Zur Dramaturgie der 'Clemenza di Tito,'" *Österreichische Musikzeitschrift* 4 (1949), 172

Procházka, Rudolph, *Mozart in Prag* (Prague, 1892)

Proß, Wolfgang, "Neulateinische Tradition und Aufklärung in Mazzolà/ Mozarts *La clemenza di Tito*," Herbert Zeman, ed., *Die österreichische Literatur* (Graz, 1979), 379–401

Raeburn, Christopher, "Mozarts Opern in Prag," *Musica* 13 (1959), 158–63

Rice, John A., "Emperor and impresario: Leopold II and the transformation of Viennese musical theater, 1790–1792," Ph.D. dissertation, University of California, Berkeley, 1987.

"Sense, sensibility, and opera seria: an epistolary debate," *Studi musicali* XV (1986), 102–38

Rochlitz, Friedrich, "Verbürgte Anekdoten aus Wolfgang Gottlieb Mozarts Leben," *Allgemeine musikalische Zeitung* 1 (1798–99), several installments from col. 17.

Sadie, Stanley, *Mozart* (London, 1965; 2nd edn. New York, 1970)

"Mozart's last opera," *Opera* 20 (1969), 837–43

"Mozart's last opera and its origins," program note to recording of *La clemenza di Tito*, Deutsche Grammophon 2709 092 (1979)

The new Grove Mozart (New York, 1983)

Schreiber, Ulrich, "Between 'porcheria tedesca' and 'true opera': the origins and fortunes of Mozart's 'Titus,'" program note to recording of *La clemenza di Tito*, Philips 6703 079 (1977)

Smith, Erik, program notes for recording of *La clemenza di Tito*, London OSA 1387 (1968)

Smith, William C., *The Italian opera and contemporary ballet in London, 1789–1820* (London, 1955)

Tyson, Alan, "'La clemenza di Tito' and its chronology," in *Musical Times* 116 (1975), 221–37; reprinted in Tyson, *Mozart: studies of the autograph scores* (Cambridge, Mass., 1987), 48–60

Volek, Tomislav, "Über den Ursprung von Mozarts Oper 'La clemenza di Tito,'" *Mozart-Jahrbuch* 1959, 274–86

Wagner, Richard, *Oper und Drama*, in *Richard Wagner: Dichtungen und Schriften*, ed. Dieter Borchmeyer, 10 vols. (Frankfurt am Main, 1983), VII

"Über die Anwendung der Musik auf das Drama" (1879), in *Richard Wagner: Dichtungen und Schriften* IX, 324–42

Wandruszka, Adam, "Die 'Clementia Austriaca' und der aufgeklärte Absolutismus: Zum politischen und ideelen Hintergrund von 'La clemenza di Tito,'" *Österreichische Musikzeitschrift* 31 (1976), 186–93

Leopold II., Erzherzog von Österreich, Grossherzog von Toskana, König von Ungarn und Böhmen, Römischer Kaiser, 2 vols. (Vienna, 1963–65)

Wangermann, Ernst, *The Austrian achievement, 1700–1800* (London, 1973)

From Joseph II to the Jacobin trials, 2nd edn. (London, 1969)

Weichlein, William J., "A comparative study of five musical settings of *La clemenza di Tito*," Ph.D. dissertation, University of Michigan, 1957

Westrup, J. A., "Two first performances: Monteverdi's 'Orfeo' and Mozart's 'La clemenza di Tito,'" *Music and Letters* 39 (1958), 327–35

Discography

T	Tito	*Ser*	Servilia
V	Vitellia	*P*	Publio
Ses	Sesto	(m)	monophonic recording
A	Annio	(c)	compact disk

All recordings are stereo LPs unless otherwise stated.

Weikenmeier *T*; Nentwig *V*; Plümacher *Ses*; Mangold *A*; Sailer *Ser*;
Müller *P* / Swabian Choral Society; Stuttgart Ton-Studio Orchestra / Lund
(recorded Dec. 1951; simple recitative omitted)
    Nixa (m) PLP. 550 (1952?)
    Period (m) 550 (1952?)
        (m) TE 1063
    Dover (m) HCR 5251–3

Krenn *T*; Casula *V*; Berganza *Ses*; Fassbaender *A*; Popp *Ser*; Franc *P* /
Vienna State Opera Orchestra and Chorus / Kertesz (much simple recitative omitted)
    London OSA 1387 (1968)
    Decca SET 357/359

Burrows *T*; Baker *V*; Minton *Ses*; Von Stade *A*; Popp *Ser*; Lloyd *P* /
Chorus and Orchestra of the Royal Opera House, Covent Garden / C.
Davis (recorded July 1976; some simple recitative omitted)
    Philips 6703.079 (1977)
    (c) 420 097–2 (1987)

Schreier *T*; Varady *V*; Berganza *Ses*; Schiml *A*; Mathis *Ser*; Adam *P* /
Rundfunkchor Leipzig; Staatskapelle Dresden / Böhm (some simple recitative omitted)
    Deutsche Grammophon 2709 092 (1979)

Gedda *T*; Zadek *V*; Malaniuk *Ses*; Offermans *A*; Wallenstein *P*; Gröschel
P / Orchestra and Chorus of Radio Cologne / Keilberth (recorded Dec.
1955 from Westdeutscher Rundfunk; simple recitative omitted)
    Cetra (m) LO 78 (c. 1979)

Hollweg *T*; Baker *V*; Minton *Ses*; Howells *A*; Cahill *Ser*; Lloyd *P* / Chrous
and Orchestra of the Royal Opera House, Covent Garden / Pritchard
(recorded 1976; some simple recitative omitted)
    (c) Music & Arts CD.641 (1990)

175

On film:

Tappy *T*; Neblett *V*; Troyanos *Ses*; Howells *A*; Malfitano *Ser*; Rydl *P* /
Vienna Philharmonic Orchestra / Levine (film made *c.* 1980 by Unitel,
Munich; direction: Jean-Pierre Ponnelle; some simple recitative omitted)
    Deutsche Grammophon 072 507–1 (CD Video; 1989)

Index

Page numbers in italics refer to illustrations.